MINDFUL OF THE LOVE

Mindful of the Love

THE HOLY COMMUNION AND DAILY LIFE

STEPHEN F. BAYNE, Jr.

New York · OXFORD UNIVERSITY PRESS · *1962*

FOR

MILO HUDSON GATES

who taught me about these things
while I was growing up.

Copyright © 1962 by Oxford University Press, Inc.
Library of Congress Catalogue Card Number: 62-9821

Printed in the United States of America

CONTENTS

FOREWORD, vii

I
"HAVING IN REMEMBRANCE" 3

II
"OUR SACRIFICE OF PRAISE AND THANKSGIVING" 28

III
"HERE WE OFFER" 52

IV
"WE, THY HUMBLE SERVANTS" 76

V
"MAY WORTHILY RECEIVE" 105

FOREWORD

It is any man's guess where the "Liturgical Movement" will take the Church, in the end. We are living through a time of remarkable liturgical concern and experiment. Indeed this excitement may be as significant a characteristic of our time as the ecumenical restlessness which is certainly true of us. Few Christian communities do not reflect this eager interest, in art and architecture, in forms of service, in ceremonial and devotional practice, in doctrinal emphasis. Much of it is founded on a great wealth of new knowledge of the early Church. The ecumenical encounter has begun to lead us all into unknown ranges of liturgical experience. Swiftly changing intellectual frontiers have deepened in us the wish to express our faith more adequately in our worship.

Where all this will go is still an open question. What will decide the question, I think, is the nature of the Church's resistance to three temptations which are inherent in this excitement. One is the danger of the museum mind. In a nostalgic age such as our own, we are constantly drawn backward in a fumbling hope to recapture what our forefathers had, or what we imagine they had. By this I mean something quite different from the healthy historical examination which ought to be true of the Church at all times. That return to our beginnings which cleanses and corrects is an unfailing good, no matter how upsetting it may sometimes be. But this is quite a different matter from the antiquarian spirit, which paws and picks among our archives in an impossible search for an ancient medicine to heal our malaise. We are not early Christians; the Church is not a museum; and the mere restoration of ancient practices will do us no good. The historical correctives only help to the degree that the sense of the continuity of the Church's life is strong. Where there is uncertainty about the steady, present guidance of the Holy Ghost in the life of the Church, historical study brings death in its train, and only strengthens the world's suspicion about the Church, that it is really a kind of veterans' society trying to keep alive the memory of old times.

A second danger is that of thinking of liturgy itself as an end. And this is complicated, because, in an important sense, worship is an end in itself. We worship because God exists; worship is the right and full response of the created to the Creator, of the redeemed to the Redeemer. Yet it is equally true that God does not spend most of His time in church, and that any worship which is not organically related to life in the world — related to it directly and immediately and effectively — is not true worship. Worship is not an escape from the tumbling, arbitrary realities of life; it is the best way we know of dealing with those realities. Therefore, whenever we enclose our worship in a pietistic capsule, welcoming it because it takes our mind off our troubles, so to speak, we run the risk of making it utterly meaningless as far as the world and our life in the world is concerned.

Third (and this is a particular danger for Anglicans), we face the temptation to idolatry. The incalculable gift of a vernacular liturgy, for example, brought to sixteenth-century man the opportunity to share the liturgical action in a depth man had not known for perhaps a thousand years. Not only were the acts themselves to be seen and appropriated from the outside, as it were, in our devout attendance; but now, through the "verbal mysticism" of a common language, the congregation could enter into the very performance and priesthood of the acts; a new depth of unity between clergy and laity could be established; a virile restoration of the corporate life and ministry of the Body was made possible. But how quickly this can turn into a form of idolatry! It may indeed be a very bookish idolatry, a tepid idolatry quite compatible with a theoretical monotheism. Even so, it is a worship of the creature rather than the Creator when the beauty

of the Prayer Book prose or the ordered dignity of
Prayer Book worship becomes a thing in itself, in our
eyes, to be treasured for its own sake. The point of all
this glorious language is to make it easier for the Church
to be whole and of a single eye in its offering of itself.
And the slippery idolatry of which I speak can destroy
this great end altogether, by placing the congregation
once again outside the liturgical action, and closing the
door to effective and costly participation.

These are dangers, tests, only. Even if we could, it
would be wrong to plead them as an argument against
liturgical development and experiment. What is needed
is that, at each stage of the liturgical movement, we
guard ourselves well against such temptations to anti-
quarianism and irrelevance and idolatry. These five
chapters were written to help in this necessary duty.
They are not at all intended to propose any new liturgical forms or practices, a task which it would be pre-
sumptuous of me to undertake. They are really no
more than conscientious reflections of a worshipping
Christian about the Eucharist, in which he has taken
part for half-a-century, the Christian in question being
especially sensitive to the three dangers mentioned —
perhaps because he is inclined to be vulnerable to them
himself.

The form of the Eucharist in which I have shared
most of my life is that of the 1928 Book of Common

Prayer of the Episcopal Church in the United States. The references are to the words and structure of that rite, and the quotations are from it. But I know that the particular rite does not matter too much in this. The great Eucharistic acts are the same in every true liturgy, and I believe that the reflections I offer would be shared generally by all Christians.*

The chapters themselves — all but Chapter IV — were delivered originally as lectures or addresses to the clergy and laity of the Diocese of Michigan, in April, 1961, on a foundation established most imaginatively and generously by Mr. Neil McMath, of Detroit, in that Diocese. I am very deeply grateful to him and to the Bishop of Michigan for the invitation which brought me an incentive to crystallize my own thoughts and an opportunity to share them with others within the household of faith. I offer these pages, trying to remember all that I have learned about offering, in thanksgiving for the gift of the Blessed Sacrament to us and for the immeasurable honor of sharing in the work of the Minister.

Stephen F. Bayne, Jr.

Compasrose
All Saints, 1961

* Users of other forms of the *Book of Common Prayer,* especially the English Book of 1662 and those which follow it closely, may find the footnotes helpful where the words in the text seem unfamiliar.

MINDFUL OF THE LOVE

I

"Having in Remembrance"

". . . having in remembrance his blessed passion and precious death, his mighty resurrection and glorious ascension; rendering unto thee most hearty thanks for the innumerable benefits procured unto us by the same." *

First a matter of phraseology. We shall be thinking about what the Prayer Book calls "The Order for The Administration of the Lord's Supper or Holy Communion." In calling the service by those names, the Prayer Book doubtless means to emphasize the most personal and immediate aspect of this service, namely, the reception by us of the consecrated elements. The phrase isn't a Reformation phrase particularly, for the centrality of the reception of the Holy Communion goes back to the beginning of Christian history, of course. But in medieval Christianity, it had become so infrequent an act that the Reformers rightly sought to

---

* The American Liturgy, like the Scottish, includes these words in the paragraph of the Consecration Prayer beginning "Wherefore, O Lord and heavenly Father." For "in remembrance" see Luke 22:19 and 1 Cor. 11:24, and for the following phrases compare the Prayer of Oblation and the Prayer of Thanksgiving in the 1662 book.

3

emphasize it. In the first Prayer Book, of 1549, the medieval name was still kept, and the service was called "The Supper of the Lord, and the Holy Communion, commonly called the Mass." But the title "Mass" was so disliked in Reformation England that it disappeared almost at once; three years later, in 1552, the present title was adopted.

I think it is good for us deliberately to use many titles for this service, for there are many sides of it to which different words refer. The word "Mass" perhaps is the most meaningless of them. It is simply a bit of medieval slang, arising from the ancient dismissal at the end of the service, when the deacon cried out to the people *"Ite, missa est"* — Go; dismissed!" Originally it did not refer to the Holy Communion alone, but to any service. To this day, it is so used by the Swedish (Lutheran) Church, to describe whatever the principal service is — *"hogmässa."*

Like many another, "Mass" became a "loaded word," especially to the people of the Reformation, for it seemed to stand either for all the medieval abuses (and therefore should be done away) or else for the true and unchanging and ancient rites (and therefore should be kept). I do not much care one way or the other; I speak of "Christmas" without many qualms . . . but I must say that, to me, some of the other titles are far richer in meaning.

"Eucharist" is doubtless the oldest of all the words, for it means simply "thanksgiving," and it stems directly from the Last Supper when our Lord took the bread and the cup and gave thanks for them. The whole service is our thank-offering for our Lord's gift of Himself; and it is hard to imagine any more fitting title.

Another of the very ancient words, another Greek one, is "Liturgy." It means "service" or "ministry" or "work." In classic Greek, a good citizen could be said to render "liturgy" to the state. In the Greek Old Testament it was used about the work of the priests and Levites in Tabernacle or Temple; and so it came into use in the New Testament, and finally came to describe the principal service of all, the Holy Communion. But when we use it, we ought always to remember its wider meanings. To speak about a "public servant" or a "minister" is to use exactly this word. The Holy Liturgy is our greatest ministry or service, but it is not the only one: every man has his ministry and service too.

Two more titles should be mentioned, at least. One is "Sacrifice" — the "Holy Sacrifice," "our sacrifice of praise and thanksgiving." The concept of sacrifice — the very word itself — is somewhat strange to our ears, for we have moved far away from a religion of animals or fruit or grain offered at God's altar. If we use the word now, we use it somewhat shamefacedly, usually, to refer to a money gift; or else it may have unpleasant associations of parents with a grudge, who have "sacrificed themselves for their children," or wives who have sacrificed "the best years of their lives" for unworthy husbands. Nevertheless it is a good word, and one which was very central and clear in our Lord's mind.

Finally, let me add the word "mysteries." This is another ancient word, seldom heard now except among the orthodox, who still use it for the Holy Communion — indeed for all "sacraments," as we call them. A "mystery" could be defined as an act of God which we can use and share, without understanding it or seeing it as God understands and sees it. There is a healthy humility about this word which makes it, too, worth remembering and using.

Well, there are seven titles, each one stressing some aspect of this great service — Lord's Supper, Holy Communion, Mass, Eucharist, Liturgy, Sacrifice, Mystery. I shall use them all, to emphasize this or that aspect of the Blessed Sacrament; and I commend the same freedom to you. Like a good many other words, these are part of a Churchman's birthright. Let them enrich your thought and prayer.

Second, I want to say a word about these chapters. All I mean to do is to take five of the great acts which make up this service, and think a little about each one. The Liturgy isn't really a made-up service of worship, such as Morning Prayer might be termed. It is an act, a series of acts, rather, a series of things done. They are done by us — by the people. They are done by the minister who celebrates the Liturgy. Mostly, they are done by Christ, Who is the real minister of it. But they are acts, things done, not words said or prayers repeated or music sung.

The whole meaning of the service depends on our understanding this. If you think of it simply as a man-made construction of devotional phrases, you cannot even begin to understand it. It is the acts, the things done, which give it all its meaning — remembering, sacrificing, offering, giving thanks, sharing in Holy Communion, going out into the world. And do not press too closely the question of who does these acts, because it is impossibly difficult to tell. Sometimes it seems like the priest, sometimes it seems like us, some-times we don't know who is doing these things, some-times it is clear that Christ is doing them.

"Having in remembrance his blessed passion and precious death, his mighty resurrection and glorious ascension" — this is the phrase I start with. And the key word in it is "remembrance." The word comes, of course, from St. Paul's first letter to the church in Corinth (I Cor. 11:24f), where he is describing the teaching he had himself received about the Liturgy. St. Luke also uses the word in his account of the Lord's Supper; he remembers that our Lord had said it as He gave them the bread, "This do in remembrance of me" (St. Luke 22:19).

Let me begin by thinking about memory as we know it. It is almost the most characteristically human act of all, I think, for it is by memory that all our various thoughts and experiences are held together at one time. So we are single persons and not simply a string of different things that happened at different times. I don't presume to know what other animals think about this; we don't necessarily have to think of them as completely and radically different from ourselves; but still we never were anything else (at least we don't remember it if we were), and so it's hard to be very doctrinaire about them. But nevertheless, I think I see something of this ministry of memory in a dog, for example. He is what I would call a "higher animal," not just because he is nearer the human level (which is simply begging the question), but because he is more of a something than a worm is.

I should be surprised if a worm had any memory at all. Perhaps he does, and when he is chopped in two, he wanders around with a split personality, hankering after the days before he had his nervous breakdown. But dogs certainly do have nervous breakdowns — at least you can induce one in a dog. And you do it precisely by abusing his memory, such as he has. You train him to remember an act and a consequence — to push a button, say, and get a bone. Then you switch the apparatus so when he pushes the button, he gets squirted with ammonia instead. This is not only a dirty trick on the dog, it is also a painful instance of the part memory plays in individuality; for the dog simply goes to pieces after enough of this deceit. He stops being an individual, and becomes a collection of whimpering, shaking fragments. Memory — such memory as he had — was what kept him sure of his own identity, and when memory deceived him, it destroyed him.

Now I will leap from dogs to us. Exactly these same things are true of us, only on a much larger scale because we are more complicated animals. A man can fight back a lot longer, for example. He would not necessarily go to pieces as fast as his dog, at least at the button-pushing level. But memory still serves the same purpose, if at an immensely deeper level. It is man's memory, his capacity to recall vividly things which have happened and hold them in his mind together with things which are happening or may happen, his power to recall people and re-establish a living conversation with them in his mind — it is this quality perhaps, more than any other, which gives him his identity, as a particular individual, separate (to some degree at least) from every other individual. And when memory deceives, we are lost, disoriented, without direction or horizon.

Of course memory isn't the only thing that enters

into this. There are two others, at least. One is the clear
sense of "now" that we have, the fleeting awareness of
this *immediate* present, this knife-edge of consciousness
that passes dizzily into memory so we can hardly catch
it, yet we know it as it passes, and know it to be different from memory. How different? Chiefly because it is
real, in the sense that what is remembered is not real
until we do something with it. As I write these words,
there is a moment when the word itself becomes present, in my mind, then on the paper; and I know the
difference between the word as I imagine it and choose
it, and the word as I write it down, and then the word
as I look back and read it, and perhaps remember the
choosing and the writing of it. There is a clear difference between the three stages of that word — imagining, writing, reading. I can recall the word and the
choosing and writing of it, and it becomes again something of the present as I recall it, or it could even become
part of imagining a future new word. But I can't rewrite
that word, or rethink *that* thought. I know the difference between the "now" and what is past and done, and
I can't possibly erase that difference.

Just so do I also know the difference between what is
imagined or hoped or awaited, and what is remembered.
Words aren't very good examples of this, because the
minute we think about the future we put words to it
(because it is so hard for us to think without putting

words to it); and then the word itself becomes part of our "now" and then immediately slides into the past, to be remembered. You can remember a hope, in other words. But as I know the sliding, dissolving present and the suddenly motionless past, so can I catch the sense of what may be, of that mysterious future which is really part of my present, as I imagine it, and so part of my past, too.

All that matters in this is that while we can speak of past, present, and future — of remembering, of present consciousness, and of imagination — as separate activities of ourselves, it is very unreal and theoretical really to try to divide them one from another. Our past is always being caught up in our present; we are what we remember, in large part. And we are also what we hope and imagine. And all these are included in the moment of present consciousness, which instantly becomes something remembered. . . .

There isn't any great point, I think, in trying to keep them too clearly separated. In fact, the main point probably is that you can't separate them completely. Time isn't quite that final, perhaps, that it can lay its hand on everything we think and are. We keep bulging over the top of time; otherwise there would be only the infinitesimal knife-edge of the now, the present, and life would be like a sort of jerky moving picture, with each frame separate from the next, and with only one showing at a time. And that isn't at all the way it is, as we well know. The present includes the past. It includes the future too.

But for the moment, let me leave this, and think a little more about memory itself. We moderns are likely to do just as I did — start with the self that remembers, as if the remembering self were all there really were to it.

The ancients had quite a different sense, and I think a deeper sense, of memory. The Old Testament reflects this deeper sense a good many times. Absalom built a pillar in the king's dale, "for he said, I have no son to keep my name in remembrance . . . and it is called unto this day, Absalom's place" (II Samuel 18:18). When Amalek fought against Moses and was defeated, the Lord said "Write this for a memorial in a book . . . for I will utterly put out the remembrance of Amalek from under heaven" (Exodus 17:14).

If the name should be forgotten, then the people themselves would perish. So Joshua prayed (Joshua 7:9) that God would prevent the Canaanites from surrounding Israel and cutting off "our name from the earth: and what wilt thou do unto thy great name?" So God used Jeroboam, an unworthy King of Israel (II Kings 14:27), so that God did not "blot out the name of Israel from under heaven: but he saved them by the hand of Jeroboam." Indeed the darkest curse of the Psalms (109:15) is that God "may cut off the memory" of the wicked from the earth.

Here is something a good deal more complex than simply the ability of an individual to recall what happened before now. The recalling is still there, but it is much more than one man's act — it is the perseverance of a person in the memory of many persons, in a group. The name of Absalom, the childless man, must somehow be remembered through the monument he builds, or else Absalom will somehow disappear. The name of Israel must be remembered on the earth, or Israel will disappear.

Something very like this, I imagine, is hidden in the cult of ancestors, as in the classic religions of the Orient. The shrines of the ancestors of the race in Japan are holy places indeed, because there they are remembered, and they live in the memory of those who attend the shrine. The Chinese family does not "worship" its ancestors, as it used sometimes to be said — they remember their ancestors, in a kind of communion of the departed, and so the living tradition of a family continues.

One of the earlier Anglican bishops in Africa says of the ancestor cult among the Ashanti, "the important thing to be noticed about this cult . . . is that it in no sense seeks to raise the (ancestors) to the status of gods. . . . It is rather a recognition of the essential unity of all members of the clan, living and departed." And a commentator says "to remember is a fundamental word in this theology. Adam had to remember, against his will, his guilt, and when the African hears of the Christians' God, he 'remembers,' at last, what was there, half-forgotten, all the time . . . the stories of Genesis offer more to the African preacher . . . (he) and his flock 'remember' that they are part of that which was from the beginning." (Bengt Sundkler: *The Christian Ministry in Africa,* pp. 289–90, 286.)

This is a far deeper sense than the merely individual and psychological sense of memory. It is less familiar to us because we have so deeply lost the feeling of any such common life. Yet even with us, there are moments when we catch this deeper sense. How much of our patriotism, for example, is really a sharing in a corporate memory? I never knew my ancestors who fought in the American Revolution — I know only their names. Yet I was, I am, somehow involved in the Revolution; and in moments of patriotic feeling, I am caught up in something far greater than anything I myself can remember. So it is in religious matters. A church service is far more than merely an individual participation. The "Communion of Saints," as we call it in the Creed, is in many ways an exact parallel to what the primitive African recognized as "the essential unity of all members of the clan, living and departed." Church rituals perpetuate that sense of communal memory. Few priests have ever celebrated the Holy Communion without feeling, dimly at least, the sense of all those myriad predecessors who have said these words and done these things and walked these slow steps.

I am not pleading for any magical interpretation of "remembrance" here. I haven't any theory about this; I am only trying to dissect out the various meanings memory has with us. The individual sense is one, surely — that way in which memory works to hold us and all our separate experiences in one piece. The communal sense of memory is also extraordinarily deep — that sense in which the identity of a group perseveres in the remembrance of those who come after — that strange longing for the persistence, the safekeeping of a name.

There is still another sense, very deeply Biblical. That is the way God remembers. He remembers Hannah in her childlessness (I Samuel 1:19); Jeremiah prays that God will remember him and visit him (Jeremiah 15:15); God remembers all Israel's wickedness (Hosea 7:2); He remembers His Covenant (Genesis 9:15), and sets a bow in the clouds in token of it; He remembers His mercy and truth toward the house of Israel (Psalm 98:3).

When God "remembers," clearly something much more is happening than a simple recalling of past events. When He remembers Israel's wickedness and the sins of his people, the guilt of those sins suddenly lives again. When He remembers His Covenant with Israel He is not merely reminded that once He promised. His remembrance brings the very Covenant itself into existence, gives it substance and reality. God's remembrance is the bringing into the present of what might once have been thought of as in the past. God's remembrance is the infusion of eternity into what time had once held captive. It is a bringing to life again of what had been dead, at least in men's eyes.

This is surely the most profound Biblical sense of memory. For that matter, it is the most profound intuition we have. "Remember thy servant, O Lord, according to the favour which thou bearest unto thy people . . ." so runs the lovely prayer in the Burial Office, which expresses for us almost our deepest feelings about the faithful departed. And while the prayer itself is a modern one (1928), the note of memory comes from the Old Testament, from Psalm 106:4, "Remember me, O Lord, with the favour that thou bearest unto thy people: O visit me with thy salvation; That I may see the good of thy chosen, that I may rejoice in the gladness of thy nation, that I may glory with thine inheritance." It is ancient; it is Biblical; yet it is completely true to our own deepest longing that

God will hold us in His loving Self, that we may live in the company of all those He has remembered and loved.

These are three, at least, of the ways memory works in our lives and minds. I dare say that all three of them were in Our Lord's mind when He said, "Do this in remembrance of me." Surely He did not mean merely that He hoped His disciples would not forget Him, and that if they would go through this little ritual, it would be a way of reminding them that once He had been with them. I doubt that this was more than a passing and even accidental meaning; it was inconceivable that He might be forgotten.

No, clearly there were deeper thoughts here. "Do this in remembrance of me" meant, first of all, that in the repetition of this act, they would reassert their identity with Him, and so be recalled to their own true selves again. We understand this well; we are sometimes saved, in a moment of great temptation, or sometimes awe-inspired, in a moment of great exaltation, by the memory of someone we once knew and loved, and have lost awhile. We remember what someone did or said; we remember the example of someone we revered greatly; and the memory saves us, strengthens us. It recalls us to ourselves again; it restores a forgotten perspective or a lost wholeness to our life; it heals and cleanses. And this is so common an experience that it is quite impossible to imagine that it did not speak quite as clearly to the first disciples and their Lord.

When they repeated this act, the brotherhood which had taught them and brought them everything they knew and had, would live again. Even when it was broken and He was gone and they were scattered, still it could be brought to reality again, to purify and strengthen them. And so it was, and so it is. The remembrance of Christ in the Lord's Supper does this for every one of us. It recalls us to Him and His example and teaching, and we are judged, shamed, lifted up again, comforted, invigorated — all this by the memory which restores a lost identity and wholeness to our selves. We are not our true and full selves when we forget Him. It is the recalling of Him which gives us back ourselves.

This is surely the first depth of meaning to find in "remembrance." But there is more. This was to be a collective act, not merely an individual service. The brotherhood was to gather, over and over again, and do this. And the lost self which was to be restored was a collective self as well as an individual one. The Church was to be cleansed and restored; the whole Body was to share in this act and so proclaim its true nature. Indeed, the act was a means by which the Church itself would continue to exist. Like Absalom's pillar, the Church had this monument which down the ages would keep its true nature before the eyes of the unbelieving world. If you would know the name of these strange people, look at what they do — they are a brotherhood gathered around the table of their Lord, who continued to keep their identity with Him, who by this solemn, corporate remembrance of Him, show Him forth to the whole world. St. Paul's phrase was "as often as ye eat this bread, and drink this cup, ye do show the Lord's death till he comes" (I Cor. 11:26).

This is a second sense of remembrance — this corporate act which recalls the Church to a true sense of its own nature, and thereby witnesses to the world what that nature is. Perhaps I can illustrate this sense by a childish reminiscence of my own. Like all choirboys I suppose, I used to have to kneel through the administration of the Holy Communion to a congregation. Our congregation was large; and the administration took a long time; and therefore we unconfirmed lads were sometimes hard put to it to find things to think about.

I remember one Sunday morning when my eyes turned to the long row of people kneeling at the Communion rail. For some reason, I began looking at the soles of their shoes. And it was an extraordinarily moving sight, to me even then. These people, so many of whom I knew as giants and moguls in the congregation, were amazingly and secretly different, when you saw the soles of their shoes. There was a sort of anonymity about it, for one thing. But the moving reflection came as I noticed the differences. A pair of new shoes would be revealed next to an old, worn pair. There were holes in some soles, and some others had patches, and some were still of the color of new leather. Some were large and some were small. Some were stylishly narrow — others were broad and heavy.

And all this simple fraternity of the shoes seemed suddenly to be a religious thing. Here was a moment when earthly differences didn't seem to matter. Here was a place to which people came, quite without regard to their differences, brought together in an astonishing unity around something that was bigger than any of them. So my childish reflection went; and so it still goes, for I have never forgotten it.

I suggest this simply as an unimportant parable of a sense of remembrance. It is precisely this brotherhood and humble, loving equality at the table of the Lord to which the Church and the world alike are continually recalled by the remembrance. It is easy for us to forget what the unity of mankind is really like. The world is quick to erase the impression worship makes on us. But day after day, week in and week out, the Eucharist placards an unfailing remembrance of humanity's real nature in Christ. We can never quite forget what we are, for the Holy Communion continually reminds us.

Or again, I remember a very vivid incident of only a few weeks ago. I had the privilege of taking part in the inauguration of the new Province of Uganda, the latest of our Anglican churches to come into independent existence. Part of the celebration of that birth was a Eucharist in the Cathedral in Kampala. Literally thousands of the faithful members of that Church came to receive the Holy Communion, and it was my privilege to be one of the ministers to distribute the Blessed Sacrament. This again was a memory which will never leave me. For here were these hundreds of Africans, with their hands outstretched to receive the Bread. I could not communicate with them, for the language barrier lay between us. My life, my culture, my background were totally different from theirs. I was only too keenly aware of my limitations as a provincial Westerner, separated from them by a thousand factors over which I had little control.

Yet the unity of the Church was perfectly clear; and it was a unity established not by words or constitutions or formulas, but by Bread. This was the basis of the unity. As their hands reached forward to hold the Bread, so did mine; and somehow our differences began to disappear, in the enormous and wonderful and somehow frightening unity of the Bread. I don't know whether this remembrance can communicate to anybody else what it does to me. But I know that I shall never forget the way in which I was recalled to a true sense of the unity of Christ's Body — the way in which the Church remembered its real nature — in that simple act.

But the deepest sense of remembrance is hidden in the act of God, and not of us at all. If Jesus were simply a good, dead man, then all the Lord's Supper could mean would be that we recalled the things He did and said, and corporately or individually rededicated ourselves to Him — to His memory, and to the trust of His teaching which we have inherited. I think it is fair to say that this is the meaning of the liturgy to many who share in it. It is an act of recollection — it is a little pageant re-enacted in order to stir within the worshippers a renewing and invigorating memory of one now long gone. It is an act by which we reach out of the now into the past, to re-establish in memory what once was true. I do not scorn that theology; I would feel that it was entirely true and helpful as far as it goes. But it does not go very far.

The point of the Christian religion is precisely that Christ is not a good, dead man, but that He reigns "at the right hand of God, in the glory of the Father." It is a living Lord Whom we follow, not a dead hero. And this changes the whole character of eucharistic remembrance. It is far more a case of God remembering us than of our remembering Him. Our remembrance is simply a way to open a channel to God, and to claim His remembrance; the important thing is that He meets us in our remembrance, in His own gracious presence and activity.

When God remembered His old Covenant with His people, then suddenly that Covenant became alive again — remembrance was the bringing into the present of what had been forgotten, had been relegated to the past. Just so is the remembrance of Him in the Holy Communion a doorway into the present, into the eternal.

Jesus is not a good, dead man. His love is not simply something to be remembered. It is an eternal fact about God. The Cross is not simply something that happened to Jesus of Nazareth 2000 years ago — it is a present description of God's love as it is. The ethical teaching of Jesus is not simply part of the biography of a great first-century teacher — it is the will of God now.

And remembrance is the act by which all this comes true, in the here and now. It isn't merely that because we remember it, therefore it becomes fresh in our minds. What happens is that our remembrance of it makes it possible for God's remembrance of us to take hold of us. Our memory is the gateway through which God enters, to re-establish His Covenant with us and open His love to us.

"Do this in remembrance of me" perhaps could be far better stated as "Do this so that I may be with you again. Gather once again at the table, say these words, break this bread and eat it, drink this cup — I will be with you." This is the full meaning and depth of the remembrance Christ enjoins on us. It is the doorway into His presence.

Let me close with three practical suggestions growing out of this. First, in our Prayer Book liturgy (as in all classic Christian liturgies), we specify certain acts of God as being those which we should remember, as we celebrate these holy mysteries. "Having in remembrance his blessed passion and precious death, his mighty resurrection and glorious ascension. . . ." These are the specific acts which constitute the heart of our corporate remembering.

I think it is fair to say that this is only a partial list of what should be remembered. In some of the ancient liturgies, as in some of the liturgies of the Orthodox Church to this day, the list is far longer. It may even start with creation and go through the whole of the Old Testament history. It may include the saints of the Christian dispensation, and the thankful remembrance of the way God continues to guide His Church all through history.

Subject only to the practical necessities of a corporate form of worship, all this seems to me very wholesome and good. In the orthodox liturgies as in some of the ancient ones, time is of little concern; and the solemn recitation of what is being remembered might well continue at great length. Our Western European habit was one of brevity and compression. Therefore our liturgies became increasingly austere and bare. But the individual worshipper may well contribute what is lacking from the words of the service. In our preparation for the Holy Communion, in our meditation about the liturgy itself, in our afterthoughts, at all times we ought to remember all of God's mighty acts, and to remember how, in such a wonderfully complete way, they are summed up in Christ. God has never failed to act in history, nor will He. It is good for us, then, to be unfailing in our remembrance of this unfailing action of God.

Second, our remembrance must include the sins of mankind as well as the gracious acts of God. We shall not remember our sins thankfully; we shall not dwell on them morbidly. But interwoven with the whole of God's activity and revelation is the tragic story of man's hardness of heart and disobedience. And in a curiously deep way, all this is interwoven with the revelation of God. We are men and not gods — therefore we are imperfect. We are men and not merely dumb and unresponsive creatures — therefore we can answer to God or fail to hear Him, we can obey or disobey. Therefore, because it is to us that God speaks, and in us and among us that He acts, we enter into the revelation, even by our disobedience. We play a part in the work of God, and supremely in the passion of Christ. Therefore our remembrance must be a two-edged sword.

Finally, the Eucharist is far more than merely a memorial of the passion and death of Christ. His whole life is the eucharistic pattern. The Last Supper, indeed, is set firmly in the context of His suffering and death. The enormous solemnity of Calvary lies behind every eucharistic word and act. But just as His self-offering on Calvary in a sense summed up His whole life of offering, so does the Eucharist sum up the whole pattern of His life. He offered, not once but continuously — therefore we share in that life-wide offering. He loved, not once but always — therefore we appropriate His love at every point of His life and of ours. The deep brotherhood of the Eucharist is not something which simply gathered around the Cross, it was a brotherhood to which He steadily invited, and invites, all mankind, at every moment. The sharing in His Body and Blood, while it is an act finally established and ratified by the Cross, is a nourishing and loving relationship which was true of Him from the very beginning, as we can see looking back from the altar to the Gospels.

His life is the eucharistic pattern. Or, to say it another way, when we share in the Eucharist, we are re-enacting everything that is true and important about Christ. In so doing, God willing, we are opening a way in which Christ can reproduce Himself in us. This is a central way in which He becomes contemporary; and it is the final point and purpose of the remembrance.

"Our Sacrifice of Praise and Thanksgiving"

"And we earnestly desire thy fatherly goodness, mercifully to accept this our sacrifice of praise and thanksgiving."

The word is "sacrifice." It is one more of the "holy" words we grow accustomed to within the Church. It has its proper and appropriate place in hymns, in prayers, in sermons, but it may be doubted whether it often has any very clear meaning in our daily life, at least as far as it relates to God. When it is used in a prayer or a church service, we understand that it refers to the religion of the Old Testament, or in some mysterious way to Christ. But this use of it has rather little meaning as far as we are concerned.

If we use the word, we very likely use it to apply to the cost of our doing something — generally somewhat unpleasant, which yet we do because we feel it is our duty. We make a "sacrificial" pledge to the Church, by which we mean that the amount of our subscription is large enough to hurt (or ought to be that large). Or we refer to the "sacrifice" we make for our children, in order that they may graduate from a good university or meet the best people or whatever.

When we use it in some purely personal connection like this, I think we are always aware that it is an ambiguous word, and sometimes a dangerous one. The sacrifices we make for our children's education, for example, may be no more than a means of propping up our own self-respect, or our esteem among our neighbors. Or when a wife speaks of how she has "sacrificed" the best years of her life for an undeserving husband, this may be often no more than a stick to beat him with.

But we also use the word, sometimes in even very secular connections, to indicate a real depth of love. We speak of men who in wartime sacrificed their lives for their fellowmen. Or we know men and women in public life, who give their time and their talents freely and altruistically, and we rightly use the word "sacrifice" to describe this.

When we use the word this way, with all its dangers, we are still remembering, although imperfectly, a true sense of the word sacrifice. The essence of any sacrifice is that it costs something real. A sacrifice is a loss of something, it is a giving-up of something, it is a death of something. All this is true; and while we often do abuse the word, by using it in shallow and selfish ways, nonetheless there is a deep memory in mankind of what it once signified, and still ought to signify.

Our basic problem, I think, is that we use the word in two quite different connections, without building

any bridges between them. If we use it about ourselves
— our jobs, our money, our children, our fellow citizens
— the word still has bite and meaning. If we use it
about God or about religion, the word seems to have
very little sense of reality to it at all. It is simply one
more of the "holy words." What I chiefly want to do
in this chapter is try to connect these two separate uses.

For our religion really is built on the assumption
that the two uses of the word are connected. The whole
furniture of our church is sacrificial. The chief object in
our church buildings is also the central object of sacrifice
— an altar. We still call it, and very deeply and rightly,
the "Holy Table," for we can never forget that our great
service began as a supper of the Lord with His disciples;
but altar it is, and altar it remains.

We speak of our clergy as "priests." And again,
while we may use many other words — presbyter,
minister, clergyman, parson — we come back in the end
to the fact that most of our clergy have been ordained
to the priesthood; and the object and work of the priest
is to offer sacrifices. Or in our devotions, we sing our
hymns about the "Saving Victim," or we speak about
Him Who is "both Priest and Victim."

Perhaps supremely, one of the high points in the
eucharistic liturgy is our prayer in which "we earnestly
desire thy fatherly goodness, mercifully to accept this
our sacrifice of praise and thanksgiving." What mean-

ing this phrase has for different people, I don't know. Doubtless some hear it simply as church language, part of the accustomed, mysterious, unintelligible vocabulary one uses toward God. Others may hear the words "praise and thanksgiving" as being of special import, indicating that the Christian sacrifice is something quite different from other sacrifices. This is, in part, what Archbishop Cranmer meant for us to do, when he translated and recombined the elements of the medieval mass, in a form which would substantially change the medieval sense. Cranmer did not coin the phrase — it is basically a New Testament phrase, and in our liturgy from the very beginning. But he intended that it should teach a new idea of sacrifice, or rather that it should destroy an old idea of sacrifice. And so it does, for many people; but let me postpone discussing this until we have thought some more about sacrifice itself.

Sacrifice — what is it? It is that unfailing element in all primitive religion, which leads men to feel that they must offer gifts to God — gifts which will please Him, or win His favor, or prove to Him our humility or devotion or penitence.

Sacrifice is the offering to God of His share — the first share — of whatever we make, or grow, or produce. It may be our tithe of money or our first son or the first bull calf or the first sheaf of grain.

Sacrifice is the common act of a people, expressed

through its priest and its temples, by which the nation comes together, in humility and offering, before its God.

Sacrifice is the priest standing on the pinnacle of the Temple, gazing toward the East, waiting for the dawn when the daily sacrifice might begin.

Sacrifice is animals, in countless thousands. One of Nero's governors, Gallo of Syria, reported that more than 250,000 lambs were sacrificed in Jerusalem each year, during the Passover. Each one had to be slain by its owner; then its life blood was caught by a priest and dashed on the altar; then it was skinned and cleaned, and part of it burned on the altar, part of it given to the priest, and part of it kept by the family that offered it.

Sacrifice is olive oil and wine and wheat, burned on an altar with incense.

Sacrifice is a goat, symbolically laden with the sins of a whole nation, and then driven out into the wilderness and over a cliff to its death.

Sacrifice is a father and mother coming with their first-born son, and offering a money offering instead, in lieu of his life.

Sacrifice was the Temple itself in Jerusalem — that vast slaughterhouse — with its enormous fire burning so that it lighted up the hills around the city, with great clouds of incense disappearing into the sky.

Sacrifice was the priesthood, that army of men who

spent their lives butchering animals, and tending the sacrificial flame.

Sacrifice is the little bunch of flowers set in a vase in front of a Hindu temple, or the little pile of stones by the side of a path in the Philippines.

Sacrifice is the rooster in Haiti whose throat is cut to sprinkle the ground. It is the martyred missionary, whose life is taken from him because of the sins of the slave trade.

Sacrifice is the Black Mass with a host stolen from a Christian altar, celebrated in some dark room somewhere.

Sacrifice is the decision to wage war, by a people no longer able to bear the sense of guilt for an unfair world.

Wherever you look in human history and human society, the elements of sacrifice are present. It is a universal impulse, and a well-nigh-universal practice. To simple, primitive people, whose emotions are as uncomplicated as their philosophy, sacrifice may take very simple and clear forms. In more complex people, who are not sure either of themselves or of God, sacrifice can become a very indirect thing indeed. But the impulse is universal; and nobody ought to try to understand very much about himself or his fellowmen, and particularly their emotional and religious life, without thinking a lot more about sacrifice in relationship to God than we often do.

Probably the most full and dramatic history of sacrifice is found in the Old Testament. What the sacrificial system of the ancient Hebrews was, when they emerged from the silence and mystery of the desert, we can only guess. Doubtless they brought with them a fairly austere and elementary sacrificial system. It may have been no more than the sacrifice of the first-born of their flocks — that ancient sacrifice of the lamb which, later on, was to become all entwined with their memory of the Exodus, and ultimately become the heart of the Passover offering.

But whatever their primitive sacrifices may have been, when they came into the land of Canaan and lodged there, they found themselves in the midst of a very luxuriant religion of sacrifice. Canaan was a settled land, an agricultural land, a land in which the constant presence and power of the local god was something continually to be reckoned with. Every high place, every great grove of trees, every strange rock was at least potentially a place where mysterious power lived. Therefore, if only to be on the safe side and make sure that whatever heavenly powers there were would be propitious toward your crop or your herds, it was far easier to let one's instincts move one toward worship. So it was a land dotted with temples and gods, a land with a sacrificial system interwoven with the daily and seasonal life of all the people.

Much of the Old Testament as we read it now has

to do with the bringing together of the religion of the land with the religion the Hebrews brought with them. Their uncompromising monotheism and their over-whelming sense of the grandeur and holiness of God came into shocking collision with what seemed to them the wicked and worldly polytheism which they found. The conflict is a deep one, and it only ends, finally, with the establishment of Jerusalem — the Holy City — as the one place where sacrifices may rightly be offered to the one God.

When the struggle was over — indeed even while the struggle was still going on — they kept looking back at their earlier history, and seeing in it deeper meanings and greater depth of meaning. This meant the rewriting of old stories and the finding of new reasons for their doing what they had done even from the beginning. And with each rewriting and each re-examination of the reason why this or that place was a holy place in their memory, or this or that act was a holy act, there came also a new understanding, and usually a deeper understanding, of what the nature of the true worship of God must be.

This was not always true. You always have to allow for the special interests of the clergy; and in any settled religion, such as the religion of Israel in its later days, the impact and influence of the professional priesthood was very strong. It was not merely a matter of their selfish interests, although those interests existed; you can't be the proprietors of the principal store of sacrificial money and animals and grain without being affected by it. But it was as much a matter of the general spirit of clericalism as it was of some particular commercial interest. The priesthood, like every priesthood, wanted to have its history neat, its reasons clear, and its position safeguarded. That's why, even now, when we read the history of the Exodus and the wandering in the desert, the description of the worship in the Tabernacle is as complicated and idealistic and impossible as it is. The Tabernacle worship represented the ultimate dream of the priestly class, of what the true worship of God was like. It is not altogether an unworldly dream by any means. But it does represent a clergyman's idea of heaven, and as such, is somewhat in need of balancing from other sides of the family.

But enough of self-examination. The rethinking and rewriting of an ancient religion was by no means always an ignoble task. For in that constant search for meaning, the great spirits of Israel, like the prophets, play their enormous part. It was the prophets who were the supreme consciences of Israel. They looked at the Temple of their day — far less rich and elaborate than the Temple of our Lord's time — and saw in it nothing but a sacred shambles. They looked at the thousands of men bringing sheep, goats, oxen, pigeons . . . and they cried out with Isaiah "To what purpose is the multitude of your sacrifices unto me? saith the Lord: I am full of the burnt offerings of rams, and the fat of fed beasts; and I delight not in the blood of bullocks, or of lambs, or of he goats" (Isaiah 1:11).

This was the voice of the conscience of Israel. The wave of sacrifice kept turning back on itself, in a constant self-examination. The impulse to sacrifice remained; yet it had constantly to be scrutinized in the light of all they knew about God. And always in Israel, there was the uncomfortable certainty that none of this vast structure of sacrifice really meant very much in the eyes of God. It was not a questioning of the principle of sacrifice; it was a feeling that "the sacrifice of God is a troubled spirit: a broken and contrite heart, O God, shalt thou not despise" (Psalm 51:17). And this uneasiness of conscience was a profound factor in the later days of the people of the Old Testament.

The ritual sacrifices went on. A man bearing a load of guilt still bought his little goat and leaned on it, leaned on it with his eyes shut trying somehow to pour all his guilt into this thing which he had bought; and then he would take it to the priest and cut its throat and pour out its life before God. But he would do this more and more uneasily, more and more wondering how he could thus transfer his guilt to something else, more and more aware that this was really something between himself and God. Yet it takes courage to break with an old system; and what your neighbors do and your fathers have done before you, you are likely to keep doing yourself, in the end.

This was the system of sacrifice, with all its enormous and glittering and bloody machinery, and with all its profound depth of spiritual insight and spiritual self-searching. This was the vast spiritual complex into which Christ came, and it is against this vast complex that we must understand what He did and said. He was never unaware of the Temple. It was for Him both the holiest of places, and the most degraded of places. The system of sacrifice which the Temple enshrined was at one and the same time a most deep and beautiful revelation of God's will, and a base and shameful abuse of God's will. It is of the greatest importance that He never turned his back on the Temple, and led the people of Israel in another direction. He did something quite different. He sanctified the Temple.

Why did He choose this way? Why did He not simply turn His back on the whole bloody, primitive, childish machinery of sacrifice, and lead mankind into a new relationship with God, based on purity of life and love? Why did He not leave us with some memorial of high ideals, rather than with this somewhat embarrassing memorial of sacrifice? These are legitimate questions, and they lie behind the refusal of many people to accept the Gospel as it is given us in the New Testament. Parts of it they will take — the Sermon on the Mount, the parables, the healings — but they will not hear of what seems to them to be a deliberate primitivism on the part of the Church.

I think He chose the way of sacrifice, and did so quite deliberately. I think He chose it for three reasons. First, the principle of sacrifice is a true principle. It is the principle that life must be released to serve its true Lord and master. Often, in thinking about sacrifice, we concentrate on the aspect of death; and in truth, there is no sacrifice without death. But the emphasis is almost always not on the death, but on what the death accomplishes. Some forms of sacrifice depend on death alone. The sacrifice of the scapegoat is doubtless one of these, when the innocent little animal is burdened with the sin and guilt of a nation, and sent forth into the wilderness to die. Here death is the major fact, for the death alone can obliterate the guilt with which it is now interwoven.

But this is rather an exception. The heart of sacrifice generally is not the death of the victim but the release of the life which, after the death and through the death, can be at least symbolically put into the hands of God to Whom the sacrifice is made. The characteristic gesture of the Temple sacrifices was not the butchering of the lambs — it was the gesture of the priest, taking the blood, the life, and dashing it on the steps of the altar or on the great curtain that hid the holiest place. This was the symbol that mattered, for it was the symbol of life offered, life released, life given to the use and glory of God.

I do not doubt myself but that this was the commanding consideration in our Lord's thought about the Passion. What was to be the sense of this death that He saw looming inescapably ahead of Him? There was no justice to it; it served no useful, earthly purpose; nor was it simply something to be accepted because it was inevitable. Nothing is more clear than that He freely chose this death. And nothing is more clear in that choice than that He saw it against the background of the sacrifice which had sealed God's first covenant with man.

In the days of Moses, it might have been enough for mankind to offer to God the best sacrifices they knew. But now a greater than Moses is here; and His covenant sacrifice must be the best and highest and fullest of earthly life, set free into the hands of God. At the Last Supper, this is clearly the symbolism in His mind — "This cup is the new testament in my blood" (St. Luke 22:20). Far from rejecting the idea of sacrifice, He carried it to its highest possible level, in the free self-offering of Man for which the prophets had for so long dreamed and prayed.

If the first consideration in His mind was that the principle of sacrifice was right, then surely the second was that the sacrifice must be appropriate to its purpose. The first covenant with Moses was sealed in the blood of oxen. This was appropriate to the law at the beginning. But the new law, the new relationship with God which Jesus had taught them, required something more than merely the ritual obedience of the old law. The new covenant was a covenant not of law, but of something greater than law — it was a covenant of grace, the seal of a new and far more completely personal relationship between God and man. And the only possible sacrifice appropriate to that covenant was the sacrifice of the whole life of man himself.

Third, this new covenant, to be sealed with the new sacrifice, was one into which all mankind must be able to enter. How often we have heard the solemn words "this is my blood of the New Testament, which is shed for you, and for many. . . ." The sacrifice was to seal the covenant not merely with those who were then bound intimately and inescapably with Him. The new covenant was for "the many" — that limitless company who in all the time to come would be added to the nucleus who shared the Last Supper with Him. The only complete and ultimate basis of human unity is humanity itself. There is no other way in which men can be bound into such a covenant as this,

save by entering themselves wholeheartedly and obedi-
ently, in and through their own manhood, into the
sacrifice which sealed it.

These, surely, are some of the thoughts that were
in His mind when He took the bread and the cup
and made them the sacramental means by which all
mankind might enter into His sacrifice and share it,
and the covenant which it sealed. And there was no
mistake in the disciples' minds, as they looked back
on the Last Supper, and the Cross, and the Resurrection. They understood precisely how it was that, for the
first time, the Victim was the Priest, and the Priest
the Victim. They understood entirely how it was that
He had opened His sacrifice to them, so that they
might share it fully. For the sacrificial death and the
life that had led up to it and the life that flowed from
it were all one; and the way you entered into the
sacrificial death of Christ was by adding your offering
of yourself to His — adding it in obedience to His law,
in abiding brotherhood, in willing and heroic love for
all mankind.

In the beginning Church there was not much confusion about Who was the sacrifice and Who was the
Priest who offered it. But it was hard for sinful men
to remember these things; it was hard for men, to
whom this sacrifice meant everything in life, not to
abuse it; it was hard for men who were commissioned

to repeat His words and His acts not to presume on that privilege; it was hard for ignorant and fearful people not to attribute to the clergy the true priesthood which was His alone. And out of this grew the familiar medieval abuses. I need not describe them. They are a matter of common history. It came to be understood by simple and unlearned people that this sacrifice was performed again and again every day at the altar. It came to be felt that there was some magical power about it. It is no wonder that one of the common words for magic is a slang version of the most sacred words in the Eucharist, when "hoc est corpus meum" (this is my body) slid quite easily into "hocus pocus." It is no wonder that, to the Reformers, the very word "sacrifice" itself became suspect. And while no Christian could ever say that the death of Christ was not a sacrifice, the inescapable mood of the Reformation was to separate man from any active participation in that sacrifice, or any seeming control over it, as far as possible.

Thomas Cranmer, the chief author of the first Prayer Book, was one of those most acutely aware of this. In his translation he took pains to make it clear that the sacrifice of Christ was in no way in man's power. It was a sacrifice once made, made "by his one oblation of himself once offered"; it was "a full, perfect, and sufficient sacrifice . . . for the sins of the whole world." Our part in it was to respond to it by adding our sacrifice of praise and thanksgiving, to receive with joy and gratitude what Christ had done for us. This is our sacrifice; this is our priesthood.

Far from questioning this, any one of us would welcome it. There can be no possible question about the unique character of His sacrifice. It could never be repeated. That imperial offering of Himself, at the very summit of His earthly life, was not something which could be put into the hands of men to re-enact magically day by day.

And what other possible response could we have to it except praise and thanksgiving? Indeed, this was true of the Church from the very beginning. The blessing of anything, in the Old Testament, is always an act of thanksgiving. Men do not presume to make things holy; God makes things holy; and men give thanks for God's gift of those things. Even at so sublime a moment as the Last Supper, our Lord does not presume to "consecrate" the bread and wine, as we say in our childish, earthly language. He gave thanks for it in the time-honored phrases of Jewish prayer — "Blessed art thou, O Lord, ruler of the universe, He that created the fruit of the vine" — "Blessed art thou, O Lord, ruler of the universe, the one who causeth bread to spring forth from the earth."

Indeed, in a far deeper sense, the whole passion of Christ was an act of thanksgiving, of joyful, free, obedient self-offering, as His whole earthly life had been. You cannot find any moment when the note of thanksgiving is absent. Nor was it ever absent from the life of the Church, from the very outset.

What confused the Reformers, as indeed it would have confused us as well, was not the introduction of the note of praise and thanksgiving. It was their feeling that you had somehow to choose — that there was something different between the sacrifice which Christ Himself had offered, once for all, and the feeble, human, moral response which alone we could make to it. The Reformers were so troubled by abuses that they lost sight of the ultimate unity which had been there at the beginning. Nobody ever really supposed that anybody but Christ could be the priestly minister of this sacrifice. Nobody ever supposed that man's part could be anything save to receive this gift of life with the most profound praise and thanksgiving. But in point of fact, people had accepted this confusion; and the magnificent, stately words of Cranmer's liturgy brought us back to a truth we ought never have forgotten. Nor ought Cranmer ever have forgotten it either.

In sum, it is our faith that the sacrifice of Christ was an event in history, deliberately chosen by Him, whereby He made, in behalf of all of us, the one perfect offering humanity could ever make. This offering can never be repeated; all we can ever do is receive it with thanksgiving. But because it is Christ Who died, because it is Christ Who is Priest and Victim alike, the sacrifice becomes an eternal and unchanging fact about God's love. Just as we thought, when we were reflecting on memory and saw that He Whom we remember is infinitely more than simply a dead man, so in His sacrifice infinitely more than merely a fact of history.

As far as time goes, as far as history means anything, the sacrifice can never be repeated. But because it is basically a fact about God and not merely about man, an unchanging truth about divine love, it is also an eternally continuing act of God. This is the way God is. This is the nature of love. This perfect sacrifice is the basic truth about the new relationship between God and man. Therefore the sacrifice is eternally being made. And into that eternal sacrifice every man can come, to add his own tiny offering of himself to the immense gift of God, in Christ. Christ is always the Victim and always the Priest. And always, from the Cross which is the altar, He holds out His arms to us to say "Will you not enter into my sacrifice, and into the covenant which my sacrifice feeds? Will you not add your offering to mine? Will you not take your life in your hands, as I did mine, and offer it in perfect, trusting, obedient freedom to the Father from whom it came?" This is surely the heart of Christian devotion.

What working thoughts come out of this consideration? I think at least these three — these, at any rate,
are the ones I find myself coming back to as the great
fixed points around which my working ideas of sacrifice
cluster.

In the first place (and this may be particularly a
thought for clergymen), we need to be careful that our
center of gravity always is in Christ's action, as Priest
and Victim, rather than in our own as we celebrate this
mystery. This is a point to which I want to return in
greater detail, later on. But it is well to be steadily reminded that Christ is the Minister of this Sacrament.
We mortals have our part. I do not disagree with the
ancient and authoritative understanding of the Church
which makes of the Eucharist the corporate act of the
Body, and therefore assigns different parts in it to different members of the Body. I do not question the need
for a properly ordained priesthood, nor the discipline
that surrounds this. All I say is that it is needful for
both priest and people to remember that all we are
doing is entering into an act which is already going on.

The priesthood of the celebrant has no meaning or
validity apart from the priesthood of Christ, Who is the
real Minister. The words which the people hear and
say, and the actions in which they join, again have no
validity apart from the great act of Christ. The words
and actions of the Church reflect what Christ is doing,

and offer to the Church a way of joining with Him in this, in our feeble and sinful human way. But we do not originate the action; Christ originates it; and it is necessary to the health of our sacramental religion — indeed necessary to our salvation — that we shall never forget this.

In the second place, Christ is Man, and it is our manhood which is offered and sacrificed in Him and by Him. One of the most deadly enemies to true Eucharistic devotion is that kind of nervous piety which exalts His sacrifice as an event so far away that it has no conceivable relationship to our simple and earthy lives. Sometimes it is an excessive, "Catholic" devotion which leads to this, born out of a fear that we may somehow sully His deity or lessen the sense of the supernatural which rightly attaches to the sacrifice. But it is not only Catholic super-piety which does this. Sometimes the most hardheaded of Evangelicals, profoundly concerned to preserve the historical uniqueness of the sacrifice, is equally guilty of leading us to forget that it is our humanity which is being sacrificed in Christ. On both sides, the danger is that the uniqueness of Christ's sacrifice will be interpreted to mean a uniqueness of His manhood. It is simply not true that His manhood is in some special class by itself. It was into *our* manhood that He came; it is our manhood, fulfilled and as it should be, which we see in Galilee and on the Cross. He is "God's idea of what it is to be a man," in a phrase of Marshall Stewart's which I shall never forget.

And because this is so, the doctrine of sacrifice becomes a binding truth about us as well as about God. The Cross and the Eucharist are facts about God. But when we look at them, we see ourselves, transfigured and transformed.

> O Saul, it shall be
> A Face like my face that receives thee; a Man like to me,
> Thou shalt love and be loved by, for ever: a Hand like this hand
> Shall throw open the gates of new life to thee! See the Christ stand!

So Browning, in most familiar lines. It might not have occurred to him that "Saul" was appropriate for an eucharistic devotion, but it is, and for most profoundly important reasons.

Lastly, both these truths, about His priesthood and His manhood, point to a third truth. That is that our sacrifice is made only through Him and in Him, and that it is our oneness with Him in all things, even in death, which supremely matters. When we come to think about offering in the next chapter, we shall have much more to reflect on about this. But it is just as well to think of this truth as one which pervades the whole doctrine of sacrifice. For it is this truth which is the root of all the warmth and sweetness of our participation in the Blessed Sacrament. All too often, in our Communion hymns and prayers, the tenderness we are led to feel seems to be rooted too narrowly in the marvelous sacramental gift itself. His immense condescension in coming among us and feeding us with the bread and the wine is an incredibly great gift, in all conscience. But there is an even greater gift here. That we are able to have even the tiniest part in His sacrifice is the greater gift. And this is possible only because He has, deliberately and lovingly, identified Himself completely with us.

It is this unbreakable unity with Him which is so wonderfully good and lovely. It can be costly, it can be even bitter, it can require of us life itself, it can disturb and remake our whole existence. But in all this, He still is saying to us as He did to the disciples at the beginning, "Come with me." And underneath all the cost of discipleship is this unchanging, gentle, tender brotherhood. At the Eucharist it rises to its full height.

The only thing we must not do, as we reflect about these points where we and He are privileged to join together, is to make the mistake of supposing that the cross we bear will look like His. It never will. Whatever our cross may be, and it will take myriad forms for there are so many of us and we are so different, the one thing we can be sure of is that it will not look like a cross. We shall never have the satisfaction, in the eyes of the world, of seeming to carry a cross. Indeed, that is why it is a cross. But only He will see it for what it is.

III

"HERE WE OFFER"

"And here we offer and present unto thee, O Lord, our selves, our souls and bodies, to be a reasonable, holy, and living sacrifice unto thee."

In the last chapter we tried to think about the whole principle of sacrifice, and the way in which Christ accepted that principle, fulfilled it, redeemed it, and made it the central pivot of His whole ministry. An essential element in sacrifice, of course, is that of offering. Indeed, from one point of view, the whole point of the sacrificial act is to offer something — more specifically to offer the life of something — to God.

Thus any sacrifice could be called an offering, and vice versa. But yet within the whole act of sacrifice, the act of offering itself is a specific thing. In the ancient sacrifices of the Temple, a man would bring a lamb from his own flock, or perhaps more likely buy one from the Temple, and he would bring it with him to the place of death. Then there would be a specific moment of offering, a point at which he took what was his and gave it to the priest. Indeed, he truly understood

52

that he was giving it to God, through the priest. The point was usually at the point of death; but this does not matter so much as that the death itself was intimately tied up with the offering. You give up what you have — you let go of what was yours — to put it into the hands of God; and the death was the final and irrevocable symbol of that giving-up. Thus the act of offering was an essential ingredient in the whole ritual of sacrifice. Indeed, it could be said to be the central act, at least from the point of view of the worshipper.

To make an offering for sacrifice was to take of what was one's own, of what had been given to you, and to let go of it, putting it back in the hands of God. A lamb, a sheaf of wheat, a first-born child . . . even though the actual offering of a child no longer was made (if indeed it had ever been part of the worship of the people of the Covenant), still a surrogate had to be found. "And when the days of her purification according to the law of Moses were accomplished, they brought Jesus to Jerusalem, to present him to the Lord. . . . And to offer a sacrifice according to that which is said in the law of the Lord, A pair of turtledoves, or two young pigeons" (St. Luke 2:22, 24).

One is tempted to reflect on this moment of offering. It was not His; it was their offering; His was yet to come. When? When would you say was the moment of offering for Him? The Cross? The night before, in the Garden? Five days before, when He brought the battle to the enemy's camp, to Jerusalem? When He prophesied His Passion? In the Wilderness, when He faced all the alternatives, and made His choice? When?

I do not suppose that there ever was, in one sense, a single moment of offering at all. For His whole life was an offering; the Cross only catches and holds in a moment of time what was always true about Him. There was nothing new about Calvary. The freedom of self-offering we see there is a familiar friend. All that is different is the finality of the Cross.

Yet in another sense, the Cross was the unique and supreme moment of offering. For true offering is not made without death. You must let go of what you offer; and death is the irrevocable letting-go, the final closing of the door to any other possibility, the end of choice.

All that I mean by this little pause is to suggest once again that it is difficult and wrong to separate His life from His death. The Eucharist is the pattern of His life as well as the memorial of His death. The sacrifice is something that went on from the beginning. "Lo, every soul is Calvary" . . . this is only a poetic phrase to describe a profoundly sober truth, that the life and death of Christ are of a piece, that what we see and rehearse in the Holy Communion is no other than the way we ought to live, that the offering we make at the altar requires to be lived out in the world.

Be that as it may, the Church understood all this at the beginning, and as it had taken over the imagery and words of sacrifice, so did it take over the whole act and concept of offering. St. Justin Martyr, a member of the second-century church in Rome and one of its greatest teachers, described an early Eucharist and its offering thus:

On Sunday there is an assembly at the same place of all (Christians) in the cities or countryside, and the memoirs of the apostles and the writings of the prophets are read as long as time allows. When the reader has finished the president (i.e. the bishop or his deputy) makes an address, an admonition and an exhortation about the imitation of these good things. Then all arise in common and offer prayers; and . . . when we have finished there is brought up bread and wine and water, and the president offers in like manner prayers and thanksgivings, as much as he is able, and the people cry out saying the *Amen,* and the distribution and sharing is made to each from the things over which thanks have been said, and is sent to those not present through the deacons. The well-to-do and those who are willing give according to their pleasure, each one of his own as he wishes, and what is collected is handed over to the president, and he helps orphans, and widows, and those who are needy because of sickness or for any other reason, and those who are in prison and the strangers on their journeys — in a word he is a guardian to all those who are in want.*

In truth, there isn't much difference in the order and structure of the liturgy from that date to our own. The Offertory — that act in which our alms and oblations are offered together with the bread and wine — remains the beginning of the actual celebration of the Holy Communion itself. Before that we have listened to the lessons from Holy Scripture and from the words of the preacher; we have joined in common devotions and in the recitation of the Creed. All this has been preliminary to what begins in the first great Eucharistic act. That act is the Offertory. I quote Dr. Shepherd: "The Offertory is our response to (the Gospel's) call, not in words only, but also in deed. In sacrificial gifts we offer back to God our entire selves, as represented by our possessions, and our bare necessities of food and drink, which are actually not our own possessions but God's gifts, and these not for ourselves only but for the promotion of the 'whole state of Christ's church' until the day when we all become partakers of his heavenly kingdom." †

But the pattern of offering was far from clear, dur-

---

* Quoted, *The Oxford American Prayer Book Commentary,* Massey H. Shepherd, Jr. (Oxford University Press, New York, 1950), p. 65.

† Op. cit. p. 65.

ing many centuries of the Church's life. Here again, as in the concept of sacrifice, sinful men were tempted, and yielded to the temptation, to abuse the pure acts of the Liturgy for their own advantage. The more the sacrifice of Christ became a remote and magical transaction, the less it seemed appropriate or even possible for men to have any share in it. This mysterious transaction was something for priests alone. The Lord Jesus had no need of what little a man could himself offer. Therefore leave the Offertory to the priest; let the Offertory become what in fact it did become, a merely ritual preparation of bread and wine by the priests and acolytes in the sanctuary, an act often going even unnoticed by the congregation.

Here, too, the Reformers reacted violently. The notion of offering involves sacrifice, and was subject to the same obvious abuses. And just as the Reformers were eager to restore the remembrance of the one sacrifice of Calvary, so were they eager to limit any sense of offering to that one, unrepeatable sacrifice. Christ's death was, as our Prayer Book says, "a full, perfect, and sufficient sacrifice, oblation, and satisfaction, for the sins of the whole world." The idea that we had any offering to make could have little meaning in the face of such determined opposition to the whole medieval understanding of sacrifice.

It is no wonder, therefore, that in the Reformation

Prayer Books like our own, the only appearance of the idea of offering is in whatever may have survived about the giving of alms. Any mention of the offering of the bread and wine on the altar disappeared from the Anglican Prayer Books in 1552. It did not return until the Scottish Prayer Book of 1637; and actually, in its completed form, it did not appear in the American Prayer Book until 1928.

The controversy which lies back of this is now largely a museum piece. We wonder that there was ever a controversy at all. But it was a bitter quarrel, for the medieval doctrine of offering had become so magical and so marked and scarred by priestcraft that it seemed to lack any sense of the Gospel whatever. The Reformers can hardly be blamed, again, for reacting so violently against a medieval abuse.

Now the current is in the other direction. We have grown very thoughtful indeed about the whole element of offering. In more parishes every year, the Offertory procession has reappeared, wherein the wardens or members of the congregation bring forward the gifts of bread and wine together with the alms of the people, so that it is clear that the whole Body of Christ, the whole congregation, joins in the Offertory act.

Less and less do we obscure the act of offering by encouraging the choir to bellow an anthem while it is going on, or by making the word "Offertory" refer only to the collection of our alms. More and more we are growing thoughtful about the whole idea of what we can offer to Him. In the ancient church, people could and did give the work of their hands to God, even to the point of making the wine and baking the bread that was to be used in the holy Mysteries. Now we feel singularly helpless about all this. Most of the time, all we can give is money. This is the universal currency that stands for man's love and skill and time; but often it seems a poor substitute for the real thing. We long to find other ways to make an offering of ourselves.

And how deeply that one phrase in the Prayer of Consecration speaks to us! "And here we offer and present unto thee, O Lord, our selves, our souls and bodies, to be a reasonable, holy, and living sacrifice unto thee." It may well be that Archbishop Cranmer was trying to lay down the law at that point about the limitations of what men could offer, in order to head off any possible misinterpretation, any possible superstition that we were offering Christ again. But whatever his motives were, the words he wrote are good and true words. His is precisely the offering we can make, of which our money is a symbol, and even more.

In sum, we are recovering the whole sense of offering again, in a deep and useful way. I quote again, at length, from Dr. Massey Shepherd, for he summarizes thoughtfully and movingly what so many of us are coming to rediscover in Holy Communion.

The Offertory is the preliminary, preparatory action of the liturgy of the Holy Table itself, a response of the Church to God's redeeming Word proclaimed to us in the Gospel and an obedience to our Lord's command to His disciples to "Do this" act of thanksgiving in remembrance of Him. It consists of three parts: (1) the bringing of the sacrificial gifts, our alms and our oblations of bread and wine, to the altar in preparation for their consecration; (2) the prayer of commendation of these gifts to God with a statement of the intention of their offering, namely, the "whole" or healthy state of Christ's Church; and (3) an act of penitence, in recognition of the imperfect and sinful account which we hereby make of our stewardship.

The offering of our alms and oblations is a representative token of the Church's use of God's bountiful gifts of creation, with which He has blessed and enriched us for the benefit of our human needs. It symbolizes, in the face of the world's selfishness and greed, the witness and sacrifice of the Church, to the end that all men may have a just and equitable share in the wealth of the earth's material goods, and that hunger and want, insecurity and anxiety for the basic necessities of life be banished from all the peoples of the world. It is significant that the offerings are made not merely in the natural forms in which God has given His gifts to us, but in manufactured forms, representative of our work and labor, and hence of all the political, social, and economic organizations of our lives. In asking God to receive these gifts and hallow them by taking them up into the redeeming oblation of His only Son, the Church performs not only an act of dutiful stewardship but also lays itself under a searching judgment. For the Offertory demands of us gifts not of convenience, easily spared, but a real sacrifice, an offering before God of a life of labor and a use of property that is devoted and costly according to His will. The spirit of reconciliation and compassion must accompany every outward offering of our substance to God if it is to be pleasing and acceptable to Him (cf. Matt. v. 23–24. 1 John iii. 17)." ‡

For the moment at least, I think we are safe from the medieval danger of a superstitious understanding of offering. At least we are safer from that danger than we are from another. There is a greater danger for us twentieth-century people, when we think in terms of offering. That is the danger of pride — of presumption.

What right has any man to offer anything to God? This is the question. In the first place, it is not ours to offer, for it is His, and only ours in trust. This is surely the deepest element in the whole idea of stewardship. And all that you and I have talked and thought and learned about stewardship has reinforced this idea in our hearts. It was not our doing that we had these gifts to make to God. We did not ask to be born, nor had we anything to do with it. We had no choice in the skills

‡ Op. cit. pp. 71–73.

we inherited or the opportunities that came to us. The generous fruits of the earth that were put into our hands were never ours. All this complex fabric of life is the gift of God. And it is a childish presumption, from one point of view, to think of offering Him what is His own.

Yet the matter is deeper than that. Of course it is all God's; and yet it is God's way with His free children to give them the power over His gifts. They may not be ours, in any ultimate sense. We cannot say, like the master of the vineyard, that we will do what we will with our own. And yet, in point of fact, we are the only instruments God has, apparently — at least in this world — to make use of His gifts. If they are not ours, still they are in our hands; we are responsible for them, and we cannot avoid that responsibility.

So there is not so much presumption on *that* side as we first thought. There is a deeper level of presumption; and we discover this level when we look at our own unworthiness to make any offering at all. We think about that perfect offering on Calvary, and how Christ's sacrifice seemed to sum up His whole beautiful life of offering; we wonder humbly and frankly at this immense gift that He made of Himself; and then, against that background, whose hands are clean? What right would I have, or you, to take anything and offer it to God? "I am a man of unclean lips," said Isaiah, "and I dwell in the midst of a people of unclean lips"; and what conceivable right would I have to stand by the side of Christ and offer my pitiful little whatever-it-is with my unclean hands?

This is the deeper problem of offering, which all thoughtful people finally come to see. I must confess that I get a little troubled sometimes, at the blithe way in which we seem to have recovered in the Church the concept of the Offertory, and the practices of the Offertory, without equally discovering the enormous sense of humility with which any such offering is made. I well remember when I, as a young man, first began to be aware of the act of offering. And how wonderfully luminous the Offertory itself suddenly became to me. I no longer thought of it simply as the time when the ushers "took the collection." I watched the priest receive the bread and wine at the hands of the acolyte, and then go to the center of the altar and lift these gifts before God; and to me it was a sudden and most moving revelation of the whole fact of offering. And how eagerly then I rediscovered the meaning of the self-offering — the "reasonable, holy, and living sacrifice" — that could be a deep secret of my own spiritual life. Suddenly my life began to make sense. It had come from God; it was my part to offer it to Him, as our Lord had offered His whole life to the Father.

I have never lost that sense; I do not want ever to

lose that sense of offering. But I had much to learn about offering. I had much to learn about my own shallow and brash self-confidence, in feeling that anything that I could offer to the Father was even worthy to be mentioned in the same breath as the offering that Christ made. My freedom was so little that I could really offer very little. There was such a thin veneer of holiness about my life, and under that veneer every kind of disobedience and uncleanness. What had I done, what had I made of what God had given me, that I should presume to offer Him anything?

But it took a long while before I came to this sense of humility. I am sure it is a right sense. I am certain that the deepest truth about offering is that nobody is good enough to make an offering to God. But at the beginning, we are likely to be so caught by the imaginative recovery of the sense of the offering and the Offertory that we may not discern the profound sense of unworthiness which must somehow cloak the whole act.

If the medieval Church lost a true sense of offering because of the way in which Christ was taken away from humanity and locked up in the hands of the priest, the contemporary Churches are in equal danger of losing a true perspective because we forget Him to Whom the offering is made, and our own unworthiness in making it. This is our danger.

How does one meet it? There is only one possible answer to this, of course. We meet it by accepting the fact that we cannot really offer this ourselves. There is not one of us who is worthy to put even the best human gifts into the hands of God. It is Christ alone Who is good enough to offer. Therefore, all our offering is "through Jesus Christ our Lord."

We saw how all this must be when we were thinking about sacrifice in the large. All I would say is that the mediation of Christ is of supreme and most urgent significance with respect to offering. It is into His hands that we put ourselves, asking Him to offer us, our souls and bodies, to the eternal Father. We hardly dare lift our eyes to heaven. We dare lift them only as high as the Cross. He Who has shared our life, Who has made Himself one even with our failures and our sin — He alone can accept what we give, and add it to His own superb and eternal self-offering.

Thus it is that Christ is in a double sense the Priest and the Victim in the holy Sacrifice. He is not only the one who took His own life into His hands and offered it to the Father. In this act which, because it is an act of God therefore is worked out in eternity, there is room enough and time enough for Him to take all that we can give and join it with His sacrifice. He is our high priest as well as His own, that is the point.

I suppose that all I am really saying is, once again,

that Christ is always the central pivot and figure of
Christian life. The man who says he does not need an
intermediary between himself and God the Father is
a man ridiculously lost and blinded in self-deceit. There
is none good enough, not one, to approach the throne
of God. Only that perfect man — "God's idea of what
it is to be a man" — only He has the right to make
the offering. Therefore He must be central in our devotion, and supremely in the Holy Sacrifice. It is no mere
piety which dictates this; the Eucharist is always His
and the sacrifice is always His, because the offering is
always His.

Now what does all this mean in terms of our day-to-
day Christian devotion? It certainly means, first of all,
deep and thoughtful recovery of the meaning and the
act of offering — all that we are presently rediscovering
about the place and importance of the Offertory in the
Liturgy. But it must also mean the humility of self-
discovery that leads us to see how unworthy we are to
make any offering ourselves. Only then can it lead to
the most extraordinary and rich and fruitful and thankful partnership with Christ. Once a man knows that
there is one who is like unto him, in all things except
sin — once we come to the point of realizing the un-
utterably deep kinship with Christ which is the privilege of every person through Holy Baptism — then the

heart of our problem here is solved. We shall go on making our offerings; but we shall make them in companionship with Him, accepting His priesthood as our own salvation, which in truth it is.

All this, about His necessary priesthood and our inescapable pride, is said most wonderfully in the final phrases of the Prayer of Consecration in the service of Holy Communion. Let me even repeat those phrases, for our better remembering: "And although we are unworthy, through our manifold sins, to offer unto thee any sacrifice; yet we beseech thee to accept this our bounden duty and service; not weighing our merits, but pardoning our offences, through Jesus Christ our Lord; by whom, and with whom, in the unity of the Holy Ghost, all honour and glory be unto thee, O Father Almighty, world without end."

These are general thoughts about our fitness to make an offering. But there are sharper questions still, which must be asked if our eucharistic devotion is to be right and true. First of all, we need to ask ourselves what offerings we actually and really can make. The Offertory — this supreme act when we come into the closest partnership with Christ — is no moment for either pious fog or unimaginative worldliness. The Offertory calls for our best. It would be better to offer nothing at all except our penitence and our shame, than to offer some trivial and casual and inexpensive tip from the surface of our life. It must be a real offering. But what can those real offerings be?

First, time and money are the universal possibilities. In an economy like that of most of us in the West, money has increasingly become the inescapable surrogate for personal service. This is by no means an unqualified blessing! Man cannot live or love or create or work out his freedom by money alone. But the fact is that with all these qualifications, money has become a medium of exchange in an infinitely deeper and richer sense than whoever invented that term imagined. It has become, more and more, the way in which we practically express our commitment and our love.

Therefore, the offering of money has been entirely removed from the area of generosity or "charity." Stewardship has become a word of the sharpest and most relevant meaning to the thoughtful Christian, not because we are idly trying to follow Old Testament examples, but because we are aware that we are trapped in a situation in which stewardship has become a commanding necessity, if there is to be any hope for us as spiritual persons. This is an inescapable part of our offering.

So is time. Money represents time; this is part of it. But far more, the offering of our time becomes more and more imperative, the more money takes the place of the personal service which once we might have been free to offer. For a money-offering alone is too easy. It is essential for us that we discipline our time as well, setting apart great blocks of time for God to command and use.

Lots of people object to "rules of life" and such mechanical things, because they say that all time belongs to God, and that there is a danger of being entirely superficial if we divide our time so meticulously, as if most of it didn't belong to God. The danger is real; every pastor is aware of the danger of a kind of spiritual old-maidishness, which delights in neat packaging of holy times. This is especially abhorrent when, as so often happens, one person's "holy times" interferes radically with somebody else's meal or sleep or holiday!

But this is not an argument against the stewardship of time, but against old-maidishness in religion. The fact still remains that a man's time has got to be disciplined, as well as his money. And what the principle of offering requires is that we shall make real and costly oblation of our time, and stick to it. And here again, it is important that we offer God only our best.

The trouble with most of us is that we divide our time the way television and radio stations schedule public interest features. The "prime commercial time" is reserved for other purposes — business or recreation.

We pay lip service by setting apart for God only those periods of time when there is nothing more exciting in the offing — the early morning, before anybody else is up — the late evening, when we are too tired to do anything else — Sunday morning, when we are comfortably in tune with the mores of our neighbors, or many of them, at any rate. Happy is that man who stops his work at noon, for five minutes of intercession. For he has learned the joy of giving the best he has to God.

Time, money . . . but what about the discipline of one's words? How much better it is, instead of blindly and stubbornly wrestling with the foul and profane word, if we learn instead to discipline ourselves positively, by deliberately and consciously seeking out the chance to use the other words. Or again, instead of dumb silence, how much better it is to take the trouble to speak, in the difficult situation. When hurt by husband or wife or friend, and an offended silence seems the appropriate response, how much more free is the Christian who makes a deliberate offering of understanding words, even though that discipline cuts across every immediate impulse in his heart. Or the casual meeting, with friend or stranger — how many of these are simply wasted, in resentment at interruption or at having to take time for another's concerns and trouble. How much better it is to turn the whole process inside out, and seize on the meeting as something that may be made a deliberate and humble, and indeed penitent, offering to God.

Friendship and love . . . is there anything here which ought not be offered? Indeed the very sweetness of friendship itself, and of love, depends on selflessness. The man or woman who wears his friends like jewelry is no friend; love is not given us to bolster our ego, but to share loneliness and find a way to break out of loneliness. And in friendship and love alike, the essential clue is that they exist for something beyond themselves. Therefore they must be offered, put into the hands of God for Him to use, for His purposes.

And so one could go on, thinking of the offerings we can make. Even pain and suffering are gifts to be offered. It is not the ugliness or the senselessness of suffering which is offered — these are as hateful and opaque to God as they are to us, I do not doubt. But the fact of suffering, the endurance which bears it, the patience and love with which it is received, the confidence and courage with which pain is accepted as something which by the grace of God one can bear, and so perhaps save another from bearing it — all these things belong to God, too. The only rule in these matters is that whatever we offer shall be something which we can imagine Christ offering. If it is something He knows and shares, if it can be found in His offering, if without hesitation we can ask Him to add it to His own, then all is well.

There are two crosscurrents to this, which ought be thought about. One is that whatever we offer must be ours to offer. This is not quite as simple a matter as it looks. We are much given to offering what is not ours, as a matter of fact. I know of families, for example, who offer their children as a kind of vicarious oblation. They mean little or nothing by their religion, themselves; but they dutifully shine their children and send them off to Sunday school, with an assurance sometimes astonishing to those who care about the Sunday school, that somehow this is "good for the children." What in fact is often happening is not that the children are being exercised helpfully, but that the parents are working off their bad conscience through their children. I don't know that I would want the children kept at home, necessarily. The point is that the children should make their own offering, and the parents another one, of their own lazy and newspaper-ridden Sunday morning.

Or again, we are likely to offer something we really don't care very much about, and which therefore is not really ours, at any great depth. I've already mentioned this, in connection with the offering of our time. But it is more than merely a matter of time. The extreme piety demonstrated at fashionable baptisms, contrasted with the somewhat lethargic church attendance of the same people, is a case in point. In such a case, the fact is that we are not really offering anything very important to God. If it is ours — if this sociable adherence to the forms of religion is ours — it is so in no very deep sense. It is really not ours at all, as much as it is a secular decoration or disguise which covers our real interests.

Or again, we will offer our non-participating attendance — our passive presence — to God. This is something often seen in church, in times when churchgoing enjoys conventional respect and endorsement. I would make one qualification here; there are times when, because of inner tumult or pain, we can offer nothing more than a passive obedience. When such times come, it is surely better to offer what we can, even though it is infinitely less than what we wish we could offer.

But I am not talking about this, but about that mood, in the offering of time, which often envelops a Sunday morning congregation. "Inspire me if you can! Change me if you will, but it will be against my better judgment! Go ahead and do what you are paid to do; I will endure it!" These are phrases which come to a parson's mind, sometimes, in beginning the conduct of public worship. What is at fault is not that the people are necessarily hardhearted, or wicked. They simply have not thought very deeply about what this experience ought to be, nor what it really is. This may not be entirely their fault, for that matter; the Church may well have failed them, in not teaching them what the true depth of church attendance is.

But here I am thinking about the conventional offering of a conventional time, in which we really are not putting into the hands of God anything that matters, anything which is really ours at all. It would have belonged to sleep, or the newspaper, or a long breakfast in the sun, or television . . . it does not matter very much, nor does it cost very much; it is not really ours; it belongs to anybody with the energy and will to capture it.

Then a second crosscurrent — when we make our offerings, we must let go of them. We must not keep them, to remind ourselves or God or our neighbors of what we have offered. If the offering is real, there is death in it; it is lost to us; it is God's to use. When our offering is money, all trace of it ought to disappear just as quickly as possible. It is a constant spiritual peril to Americans, for example, that when they fill out their income tax reports, they must go back over their generosity for the past year! I am not thereby pleading for a change in the income tax laws; I am pleading only for the anonymity of love.

This anonymity — this secrecy, which Christ so

often enjoined on us — this is a basic principle of offering. Let these things go — these hours, these dollars, these words, these friendships, these pains, these offerings of talent and skill and devotion. Let them go, for we have given them to God to use. Without this selflessness, no offering can be real or true. Heaven knows it is not easy to achieve anonymity; it would be a very bold man who ever felt he had achieved it. Indeed, this becomes part of the humility and penitence with which the offering is made. But it is death to the soul if we ever forget the necessity of the constant fight for selflessness, if we ever forget His anonymity, this secret Priest, Who offered Himself, all His time (so few years), all His money, words, friendships, pains, so silently and so unremembering. Even those who thought they knew Him best, perhaps did know Him best, did not know how completely and trustingly He let go of His offering. Yet now we know, for it is written for all to see. And it is this Priest to Whom and through Whom our confiding love bears our offerings. Therefore we can let go of them, if we will only remember Him.

I V

"WE, THY HUMBLE SERVANTS"

". . . we, thy humble servants, do celebrate and make here before thy Divine Majesty, with these thy holy gifts, which we now offer unto thee, the memorial thy Son hath commanded us to make. . . ." *

Two or three times in the course of these pages — most of all in Chapter II — we have been brought face to face with the question "who is the minister of the Holy Communion?" I am sure in my own mind that the deepest and most nearly adequate way to answer that question is to say that Christ is the Minister. I do not think that answer needs any theological defense; as far as I know, it is (in perhaps oversimplified form) the reflection of a generally accepted and acceptable theological truth. Very likely it is too simple, too com-

---

* These words in the American Liturgy, like the very similar words in the Scottish Liturgy, precede the Communion, hence the prayer that we "may worthily receive." In the 1662 service the corresponding words are in the Prayer of Humble Access ("so to eat the flesh of thy dear Son Jesus Christ that . . . we may evermore dwell in him, and he in us"), in the Prayer of Oblation ("that all we who are partakers of this Holy Communion may be fulfilled with thy grace and heavenly benediction") and in the Prayer of Thanksgiving ("incorporate in the mystical body of thy Son").

pressed. Therefore I think it might be helpful now to come back to the question once again, and look at the answer a little more closely, at different depths or from different perspectives.

First, if it is true that Christ is the Minister of the Holy Communion, what are the implications of this answer for the ordained ministry of the Church? It could have, and at times in the history of the Church it has had, devastating implications with respect to the professional prerogatives of the ordained clergy. I cannot remember very many movements of radical reformation within the Church which have not appealed to the supreme Ministry of Christ, to unseat the clergy — or at least to weaken their grip on the life of the Church. Indeed these periodic appeals over the heads of the hierarchy to the supremacy of Christ's Ministry may be quite justified, for all I know. No clergyman is likely to seek to exempt himself or his order from the charge of pride or presumption or the faithless stewardship which turns into tyranny.

For that matter, it is as likely to be the clergy as it is the laity who make this appeal. Sometimes we do it for unworthy motives. There are episodes in the ministry of most of us, when our professional qualifications are challenged or our position as the minister of the congregation is threatened, when it is very tempting to remind the congregation and ourselves that

Christ is really the Minister. In such a case, what we are really saying is that because Christ is the Minister, therefore the congregation ought to pay a good deal more respect and reverence than they are now doing, to our ministry as His deputies. I do not question the fact that the ordained clergy are in a peculiar sense the deputies of Christ. I do not believe the orders of the ministry came into existence by accident. But surely the point of the appeal to Christ is not to bolster the threatened ego of a clergyman — it is rather to help the clergyman understand his ministry in its greatest and most humbling terms.

And this is precisely what often, and most mercifully, happens. It may be, when we are young priests, that we are overimpressed with the privilege which is ours of conducting the liturgy of the Church. But I think that no priest functions very long before he is driven to meditate on the rubrics of the Communion service — particularly those which control and dictate his action during the Prayer of Consecration — and this is a somewhat explosive meditation, when it comes.

It may be that we have read those italicized words a thousand times. At some point, we read them with new eyes. "*Here the Priest is to take the Paten into his hands . . . and here to break the Bread . . . and here to lay his hand upon all the Bread . . . here he is to take the Cup into his hands . . . and here he is to lay his hands upon every vessel in which there is any Wine to be consecrated."*

We read those words with new eyes, I say, and we relate them to the actions which correspond to them. And suddenly, with an almost shattering humility, we realize how absurd our youthful, priestly self-consciousness must have seemed in the eyes of God. For none of the words or the acts was ours, at all. It is our hands that He uses; it is our voice through which He speaks; but our part in all this is nothing more than the obedience of a humble servant. Where, then, are the pretensions of priestcraft? They have been blown away by the great cleansing wind of the grace of God, and we have been led to learn that the first virtue of the priest is obedience. We should have known this all along. But it takes a bit of learning before we come to realize what the faithfulness of a steward means, or what is signified in St. Paul's description of himself as "an ambassador in bonds."

Indeed, the first virtue of the priest is obedience. And nowhere is this more movingly illustrated than in the liturgical obedience enjoined on us by the Book of Common Prayer. I don't know at all that whoever wrote these rubrics had any least idea that they were anything more than simply directions for the action of the celebrant of the Holy Communion. Indeed they are nothing more than that. But the only reason these simple directions exist at all is precisely that Christ is the Minister. If it were not for Him, it would make absolutely no difference whatever what the priest did or said, if Christ were not the Minister. It is precisely the point of obedience which is at stake here — obedience to Him Whose Ministry alone matters. In order that it be clear that He is the Minister, in order that He may accomplish His Ministry, it is absolutely necessary that the priest shall do what Christ did, and say what He said, and interject no personal conceit or private action of his own.

Of course the principle of obedience is much more than a merely liturgical one. The whole steadiness of the pastor is born in obedience. The clergyman's leadership of his congregation is born in obedience. Whatever of usefulness we are to the flock entrusted to our care depends entirely on the degree to which they can trust in our obedience. Our obedience to the Gospel, our obedience to the Church, our obedience to our Lord — these are the only certainties the flock of Christ have. These are far greater certainties, in their way, than the mere new performance of liturgical duty, of course. But, in a curiously deep manner, the greater is rooted in the lesser. In fact, I should think that the liturgical obedience is the ground and source of all the rest. If it is at all true that in the liturgy the Church sees itself as it really is, then it is really of crucial importance that the Church shall see plainly that Christ is the Minister. And the clearest way the Church can ever see this is in the obedience of its ordained clergy to Him Whose Ministry the whole Church shares.

Let me pursue another line for a moment. In our Church, the vestments worn by the clergy are at times a matter of somewhat nervous excitement. It is probably less so than formerly. But there still is a measure of tension about such things, in some quarters; and this tension becomes important at the frontiers of the Church. There are many friendly and interested and even concerned inquirers who are thrown off by the oddities of ecclesiastical vesture, or gossip about them; and when this happens — when a man or a woman has been gripped in depth by the Gospel and the Faith, only to be miserably turned aside by such a triviality — it is, and it ought to be, a matter of some self-searching on our part.

I have no intention here of getting involved in an argument about what are the correct clothes for the clergy to wear, in church. All clothing is basically ridiculous. A bishop wears a rather spectacularly curious outfit, when he has his puff sleeves on; but I have decided that it is essentially not any more uncouth than the coat and trousers of my lay brothers. The only thing is that there are fewer bishops, and not many more of the clergy, over against the whole conventional mass of the be-coated and be-trousered. But of the various kinds of eccentric liturgical dress, I say nothing.

The only point at issue, and this is a serious point, is that the purpose of vestments — their usefulness and function — is to confer anonymity upon the minister. Like the rubrics, vestments are a small thing; but they are indicative of something of central importance. And the matter of importance is, again, that it be perfectly clear that the individual minister does not really matter, that Christ is the Minister. When we clothe ourselves in surplice or chasuble or cope, it is as if we put the Church over our shoulders, to lose ourselves, our separateness, in the corporate life of the Body. It is not a perfect illusion, God knows. The individuality of the clergyman cannot be really submerged. His struggle for selflessness has got to go on; and the congregation must learn this, and help him, and be patient with him. All the same, the vestments are an outward and visible sign of one more of the cardinal virtues of the priest — a sign of his wish and prayer for that glorious anonymity expressed in St. Paul's phrase, "We preach not ourselves but Christ Jesus the Lord; and ourselves your servants for Jesus' sake."

Again, this is no mere liturgical virtue. It is perhaps supremely a virtue for preachers to seek. Preaching is one of the most delicate of all tasks. In one sense, the strength and goodness of preaching depends entirely on the personality of the preacher. Phillips Brooks's famous aphorism that the sermon is "truth mediated through personality" will remain for a long time as a sobering reminder of the fact that the preacher can by no means avoid being the vessel God chooses to use, for the revelation of His will. And yet, even in this most personal relationship, it remains true that the preacher's ultimate duty is to get out of God's way.

It is the *translucence* of sermons which matters. A speech or a lecture may be as hard or brilliant as the occasion demands or allows. Even a novel or a poem can be somewhat of two minds in this respect — they ought to communicate, but they may be permitted also to dazzle. But the light has got to shine through a sermon, or else it is no good at all. There are better speeches any day than most of us could produce, in the pulpit. But it is not the preacher's art to make speeches. The virtue of the sermon is translucence. And this is only another way of saying that Christ is the Minister.

So it is all through a man's ministry. From beginning to end, along with obedience he needs and seeks to find the skill, the humility, the maturity, the freedom, which will let him get out of Christ's way; and it is of this that the vestments, in their absurd and tiny and earthy way, speak. In themselves they do not matter

at all. But the next time you, a layman, wonder at the
strange costume your priest wears, let your mind turn
instead to the question "Who is the minister?"

If what I have just said seems trivial, then let me
ask you to think for a moment about the sources of
courage in the ministry. Where does the boldness, the
necessary independence of the ministry come from? Is
it born simply in some individual sturdiness or ec-
centricity of the man himself? I suppose it is, sometimes — the ministry, by its very nature as well as its
current social ambiance, attracts more than its fair share
of independently minded people. But I do not think
this matters very much. For most of us, who are no
more brave or free than we ought to be, the only unfailing source of courage lies not in our own nature at
all, but in the steady, nourishing awareness that we are
only a voice and hands and a heart of the One Whose
Ministry we are privileged to share.

When the judgment of the Gospel must be spoken,
the only courage the priest can rely on is his certainty
that he is speaking for the One Who is to come to
judge. When the pastor must fulfill his role of whip-
ping boy for his parish, the only place he can look for
constancy and steadiness is to the Minister. When he
must stand by the side of those facing temptation, the
only assurance he can bring them is that Christ is stand-

ing by their side. When the clergyman tries to fulfill
his teaching duty in the Church, the only right he has
to speak, and the only authority which lies behind his
words, is that which comes from the Teacher Whose
servant he is.

These are not fanciful things. These are the unchanging truths about the ministry of the Church. If
that ministry, down through the ages, had had to depend for its virile and constant courage on the human
resources of its clergy, I don't say that the Church
would not now exist; I say that whatever Church existed would have little or no resemblance to the Church
of the New Testament. In point of fact, where that
resemblance doesn't exist, it is precisely because the
Church has forgotten that the only source of its courage
is in Christ the Minister. Let the Church forget that —
let a generation come who imagine that the ministry
is merely a technical art to be learned, and that the
Gospel is simply a disguised way of talking about human psychological resources — and you would see the
end of any recognizable Church at all.

But God is good, and God is patient, and over and
over again He teaches the Church what we ought never
to forget — that the Church is His and its ministry is
His. He teaches us in a thousand ways, year in and
year out, in small ways as often as great ones, that

Christ is the Minister. And from this flows the obedience and the self-emptying and the bravery of the Church.

One is tempted to go on, to think of all the ministries of the Church against this background. Who baptizes babies, really? Who confirms? Who solemnizes Holy Matrimony? Who forgives sin? Who makes priests? Who heals the sick? In every case, we are driven back relentlessly to the certainty that it is really Christ Who is the Minister of all these sacraments. Everywhere the question is asked, the answer is the same as it is when we ask it at that supreme point in the Church's life, at the altar. If Christ be not the minister, then all our petty ministries are vain. But the faithful certainty of the Church continues. He is the Minister.

All this I believe with all my heart. But when I come to this point in my reflection, and I imagine that this is so with you too, I begin to be aware of the danger of oversimplification. And perhaps nowhere is that danger more clear than in another area — that most delicate and challenging area of the divisions within the Church. If Christ is the Minister, what are the implications of this for the unity of the Church? I cannot pretend here to do more than sketch the issues, and suggest the two moods in which we find ourselves. But let me do that, if nothing more, if only to mark off a place where fruitful confrontation and dialogue may possibly take place. Bear with me, then, if I suggest, in absurd and almost frivolous simplicity, two contrasting points of view on the question of the due and rightful place of the ordained ministry in the life of the Church.

The first view, the fact of Christ's Ministry is all that really matters. Details of Church orders and organization are entirely secondary, to be settled on a purely local or traditional basis. Perhaps the most that can or need be said for the ministerial hierarchy of the Church is that it is useful for the well-being of the Church and its better government. But such order is by no means a controlling factor, save possibly in purely internal questions. Christ is entirely free to enlist and use any man or woman for the fulfillment of His ministry, under any circumstances He chooses. All that is required (or almost all) is sincerity in Christian discipleship of the one who feels called by Christ to such a ministry.

Doubtless this is an extreme view, held in its entirety by only a few Christians. Almost all organized bodies of Christians accept some discipline as to the ministry, and require some recognition by the body as a whole. But within these qualifications, I think the general frame of mind suggested in this sketch is authentic. It is an extreme and radical statement that Christ is the Minister of the Church. Indeed, more than this is said — He is the Lord of the Church as well as its Minister. But this in no way diminishes the truth of the assertion. It only accents it; and all Christians would agree as to His Lordship, at the Father's appointment.

With this view I contrast another one, in which the fact of Christ's Ministry is not all that matters. While that Ministry would not be questioned — while indeed it would be fully and clearly accepted — the center of gravity of this second view would lie in another consideration. As in our Lord's own Incarnation, the Ministry of Christ must be carried out within time and space. The visible Church of Christ is an institution within time and space. And while no one would question the right of Christ, at any time and under any circumstances, to choose whom He would to serve Him and the Church, nevertheless it would seem both appropriate and clear that God fully accepts the limitation of time and space, in the government of the Church. Specifically, this means that questions of Church order and government are not indifferent or secondary. If the Church is of importance to God at all, then the manner of its life and polity must be of importance to Him. And if, as certainly seems the case to the vast majority of Christians, God has chosen a certain ministry to preserve the unity and continuity of the Church down through the ages, the claims of this ministry to an authoritative place in the life of the Church must be taken seriously.

Again, there are varying degrees of emphasis in this. In more extreme views, which probably few Christians hold, any ministry in Church or world which does not share this fully authoritative foundation is blasphemous or little short of blasphemous. But this is doubtless an extreme view. For most who share this understanding of the ministry, some intermediate position is probably characteristic. But all alike would hold, I suppose, that the institutions of the earthly, time-and-space Church must be taken seriously; they are of God's establishment and not man's; they are not indifferent matters to be decided as each individual or group wishes; they are acts of deliberate Divine self-limitation — indeed, acts of Divine Will.

The dangers on both sides are clear. In the first view, there is a constant danger of anarchy, and of a senseless disregard of the necessity for the Church to accommodate itself to time and space. Its characteristic heresy is likely to be that of pure spirituality — of not accepting the principle of Incarnation, and the necessary limitations of creatureliness. The ultimate end of the Church, if that view is followed to its conclusion, is either that the Church dissolves into a random collection of devout atoms, or becomes a merely human association for the furtherance of the Christian Faith and life. And neither of these extremes resembles the Church of the New Testament, which is the only fundamental guide we have. They may be defensible in purely human terms. But Christianity is an anchored religion; we are not free simply to choose whatever form or organization seems appropriate and agreeable to us.

The dangers on the other side are equally clear. Carried to its extreme, the second point in view ends in pure legalism, and in a fundamental disregard of the doctrine of Christ's Ministry. While lip service may continue to be paid to that doctrine, in point of fact it becomes a purely honorary teaching. Such a Christ, like any other constitutional monarch, reigns but does not rule. For all practical purposes, He and his Ministry are in the control of fallible men. I do not say that the Church, even at its worst, has ever quite gone this far. Certainly it has never said these things in so many words. But it may even be a worse sin that these things were not said, but that the Church lived this way.

But with all the dangers, is there anyone who does not respond warmly to both these points of view, in some measure? Although I have been brought up much more within the second point of view than the first, I must own to a good deal of sympathy with the first attitude. I think most of the clergy would agree with that. For we have seen, all too often, how Christ over-rules us, in the life of our own parish as well as the wider

Church. How often He has chosen humble members of the laity to admonish us silently, with their great faith and tireless love. How often, especially in our more dogmatic moments, have we been taught and corrected by those who claimed no right as teachers of the Church at all. No, I think any priest of reasonable experience would be quick to recognize that he has much to learn from those who hold the official priesthood in little respect.

And any honest friend of the Church must recognize how unbearable an established hierarchy can sometimes be, whether clerical or lay. We are sinful men — vestrymen and trustees as well as priests and pastors — and whenever we are cloaked with some little authority, it is likely to go to our heads. Therefore the rebelliousness of those who cry out that God is not the prisoner of the Church speaks clearly and movingly to us, except in our worst moments of controversy.

Both these attitudes are spirits, rather than settled theologies. People holding them still often differ widely among themselves as to particular questions of Church order and government. Those who exalt the absolute primacy of the Ministry of Christ still must come to terms with respect to the practical management of the Church's affairs, unless, indeed, they are content to have the visible Church disappear altogether. And on the other side, there is by no means unity among those who hold to an episcopal form of government, for example, and those who support presbyterian or congregational policy. All I am contrasting here are two moods, two attitudes, two spirits, two directions in which the minds of men tend to move.

And it is useful to make this contrast, because the two spirits are often what is at stake, at the basis of many lesser disputes within the whole ecumenical encounter. Many of the lesser questions can be answered, or could be answered, on a purely historical basis, if there were agreement on the greater issues. But as long as we fall apart on the broader grounds of our understanding in these matters, there is little hope that our dialogue on lesser matters will ever be more than a sparring match.

I do not hold any wild hopes that someday there will be agreement on this fundamental issue. Both spirits have played on the life of the Church for twenty centuries. It would be idle to suppose that, in some magical way, we could finally decide on one or the other, or even on some agreed compromise solution. The two contrasted spirits are profoundly deep in human nature; the most that can be hoped for is a fruitful tension and interplay between them.

In point of fact, this has been true of the Church, for most of its life. On the basis of twenty centuries of experience (and I grant that this is not necessarily a very long time, or a very secure basis), the Church has held together, despite these profound tensions, for a far longer time than it has suffered itself to be divided. Other matters have divided the Church — matters of political issues, of geographical and traditional differences, to say nothing of the more profound disagreements in doctrine. But on this specific issue, in the face of this particular and profound tension, it has been more generally true that we managed to hold these two points of view together, in tension, than that we fell apart because of them.

This is, to me, a source of hope. It does not seem to me a wild or desperate dream, to imagine that it is possible to contain these two spirits within one body. The very doctrine of the Incarnation itself teaches me that God — the unlimited, the spiritual, the Lord — "for us men and for our salvation came down from heaven, And was incarnate by the Holy Ghost of the Virgin Mary, And was made man." And this becoming man involved precisely what Christians must take seriously, when they speak of the Church as an institution within time and space. Just as God accepted voluntarily the limitations of creatureliness, so must the Church accept these limitations. And these limitations mean (among many other things) a deliberate accept-

ance of a particular, perhaps quite arbitrary church
order, with all its necessary apparatus of hierarchy and
responsibility, of prerogatives and duties.

But if all this is to remain in the service of God and
not of men, it is essential that there be provided every
opportunity for God to exercise His ultimate Lordship
over His Church. Thus, there must be freedom within
the Church for the kind of nourishing and healthy self-
criticism which purifies and cleanses. More, there must
be manifest a just and adequate sharing of the ministry
and a brotherly partnership within it, so that it is seen
to be the proper work of every member of the Church
in his own order, and not merely of a privileged class
within it. Most of all, the supreme position of Holy
Scripture within the life of the Church must be clearly
seen and given every ultimate protection. God has given
us no better guide to His Lordship than the Bible. As
long as it is clear that He is Lord as well as Minister,
and that His revelation in Holy Scripture is the supreme
guide and governor of the Church, we shall never be
finally or disastrously deceived by the historical choices
we must make.

But all three of these protections must be written into
the constitution of the Church, if the healthy tension
and balance between the two spirits is to be maintained.
Neither spirit must ever be suffered to win a final vic-
tory over the other. And if we are to be moved to com-

plain that this means a constant ferment within the Church, we will do well to remember that He came not to send peace but a sword. Judgment plays over the Church as well as the world, and must always be free to do so. The man who hopes for a neat, authoritative, unchanging package of the Church is bound to be disappointed. So is the romantic anarchist, who would prefer that men were angels.

Now is all this that I have written simply an aimless meditation? I hope not, and I believe not. I hold, with all my heart, to the truth that Christ is the Minister. Otherwise I would be able to see no value, but rather simple blasphemy, in the ministry I try to exercise, liturgical and otherwise. But to say this means very little if we do not at the same time remember the Incarnation, and the Creation, and accept the rigorous and humiliating limitations of being men and women, mortal, time-bound, destined to live our whole life breast deep in the urgent river of responsible freedom. You cannot have either life or God the way you want them — and can only have it, and Him, on His terms. And to accept this, within the life of the Church, means often that nobody is going to be entirely right, but that we must all live in an uneasy tension, among ourselves, even within ourselves.

It may well be that we children of the Anglican tradition ought to have a keener appreciation of this tension than anybody else. I say this not in pride, but as an admonition to ourselves. For the heart of the Anglican dream, as far as it can ever be separated from the dream of all Christians, is to be found precisely at this point of tension. When we speak of the way in which both Protestant and Catholic elements are combined in the Anglican tradition, we are not talking about easy alternative. You do not discover this tension by hunting one parish which is "Protestant" and another parish which is "Catholic" — there are not two kinds of diocese, or two Prayer Books. Indeed, you are not justified in even looking for a "Protestant" man or a "Catholic" man within the Church. For the tension is deeper than even this. It is a tension which, in our point of view, goes to the very heart of the life of the individual priest or layman.

The most "Catholic-minded" priest cannot put aside the fact of his ordination vow, "that the Holy Scriptures contain all Doctrine required as necessary for eternal salvation through faith in Jesus Christ," and that he will "teach nothing, as necessary to eternal salvation, but that which he shall be persuaded may be concluded and proved by the Scripture." Nor can the most "Evangelically minded" priest divest himself of the hierarchical order of the ministry, within which he must play his appointed part. And as it is with the clergy, so is it with the laity. They do not undertake the same obligations, nor accept the same discipline as do the clergy. This does not mean that thereby they have a lesser obligation or a milder discipline — it means only that the ministry of the laity within the Church is different from that of the clergy. But with the laity as with the clergy, the doctrine of the Incarnation, that teaching of the wonderful, gentle, self-limitation of God in coming inside our humanity, plays its commanding part. For all of us, clergy and laity alike, Christ is the Minister. He is absolutely sovereign and supreme. And His Ministry, now as of old, is expressed through His humility, in committing Himself by the will of the Father to the narrow and painful restrictions of mortality. Christ is the Minister; but it is the incarnate Christ Who is the Minister. Therefore the Church cannot escape its creaturely involvement in time and space, nor can it escape His ultimate and controlling Lordship.

Let me close this chapter with one more, brief look at Christ's Ministry — this time at some of its implications for the ministry of the laity. I quote a passage from a notable address by a lay Churchman:

Our people need to understand more fully than they do in most parishes that they come to church in order to *perform* the liturgy, not to be spectators of it. What they come for is to let Christ in them offer themselves and their world to God, united with His own one, perfect, and sufficient sacrifice. As

Alfred Shands says, "When the laity begin to realize that they are in part at least 'co-consecrators' with the priest, they will be more ready to see Christ is the only true consecrator at the liturgy, and that the priest will once again become the 'president' of the liturgical assembly. . . ." †

I need hardly say that this passage seems to me profoundly true and profoundly important. It is true to the Church of the New Testament, which is the basic test of all. But its importance does not rest only with that. What matters is that it points the way to a recovery of the full meaning and the great dimensions of the ministry of the laity.

I do not altogether like that phrase, "the ministry of the laity." I think it can be used in a slippery way, as if to say that the laity have a ministry of their own, different in kind from that of the clergy; and when it is used that way, it often turns out to be a kind of sop or pacifier, tossed to the laity from the clergy, or perhaps more often, proposed by the laity themselves out of ignorance or professional laicism or whatever. The point is that there is only one ministry in the Church, that is the Ministry of Christ.

Every member of the Church shares in this Ministry, in the priestly Body of the Church. Each of us has

† "The Liturgical Movement and the Ministry of the Laity"; Frank Stephen Cellier in *The Eucharist and Liturgical Renewal* (Oxford University Press, New York, 1960), pp. 103–104.

his own part and duties; each of us is part of the Body; and to that degree, it is right to think of the ministry of the laity as contrasted with that of the clergy. But it is wholly wrong to press that distinction to the point of seeming to say that these orders of ministry are really separate kinds or degrees of ministry. This is the "slipperiness" of the phrase.

I even question a bit Fr. Shands's cautious words (quoted above) about the laity realizing that "they are in part at least co-consecrators with the priest." Why "in part"? They are, unqualifiedly, co-consecrators with him, and he with them, and all with Christ. The difference is not in the *degree* of participation, it is in the *mode* of participation. And I think we need say this far more boldly than we usually do. If we do not, then we shall not recover and hold the essential priestliness of the life and work of the laity in the world. If they are doomed forever to a role of a sanctified acolyte or a diluted priest, then there is little use in urging a stronger lay apostolate. It is only as all of us, clergy and laity alike, face and accept the priestliness of the whole Body, a quality which attaches equally to every member whatever his particular duties may be, that we can come to the essential depth and wonder of the Church's mission in the world.

The ministry of the laity is not a different ministry — it is the layman's way of sharing in Christ's Ministry. This is what must be clear at the heart of the Church, in the Liturgy, if it is to be clear in the world.

A similar slipperiness attaches to another phrase often used in these matters — "the priesthood of all believers." In one sense, nobody could quarrel with this expression, for it is rooted in the classic and central doctrine of the Church, and is clearly established in the New Testament ("Ye are . . . an holy priesthood, to offer up spiritual sacrifices, acceptable to God by Jesus Christ . . . a royal priesthood . . . kings and priests . . .": I Peter 2:5, 9; Revelation 5:10). All members of the Body share in the priestliness of the Body.

I think the phrase tends to become ambiguous when it is used to imply that all functions within the Body are alike. This implication is utterly foreign to the New Testament; indeed it would destroy the meaning of the Body altogether, for that meaning depends on diversity, not identity, of function. More, it would take away any meaning from the idea of the layman's ministry, for his share in the ministry depends entirely on diversity of function. A layman playing at being a parson doesn't make any more sense than a parson pretending he is really a layman. We do not respect either one the more for his pretension. What is more important, such pretension blurs and dulls precisely the diversity and partnership of function within the ministry on which the witness of the Church depends.

It will not do for us to be sentimental or shallow about these matters. Christians have got to learn to hold two ideas in tension — the idea of the Ministry of Christ, and the idea of the ordered ministry of the Church on earth. And just as we saw before, so do we see once again the danger of sliding over on one side or the other. Christ's Ministry in this world depends on the diversity of ways His Church works out that Ministry. But the meaning of the Church's ministry, in turn, depends entirely on the fact that it is not the Church's ministry, in the end, but Christ's.

This is not to argue against using either of the two phrases. It is only to urge care in our use of them. All too often one finds them linked together in enthusiastic speech, as if attempting to establish a rough egalitarianism and democracy within the Church and restore self-respect to the laity and modesty to the clergy. This troubles me — not the restoration of worthy virtues, but the egalitarianism; for if this were true, then neither the ministry of the laity nor the priesthood of all believers would have any real meaning at all. And what they both enshrine, in different ways, is a most precious truth.

If Christ is the Minister, then the full, corporate,

brotherly life of the Body has reality. Both in Church
and world, if it is His single Ministry we share in our
different ways, all will be well. The ways must be
different, for the work of the priest is widely different
from the work of the layman. But the necessary unity
is given to us all, in Christ. And with the unity comes
a new sense of holiness and urgency about the tasks of
both clergy and laity. If it is Christ's Ministry at stake,
then what the priest does is invested with all the immense solemnity and glory of the incarnate Lord. If it
is Christ's Ministry at stake, then all the layman does
in the world is equally invested with that solemnity
and glory.

This is really all I want to say, or can say, I think. I
must own to the greatest respect for the task and ministry of the laity. We in the clergy are often pitied and
comforted for the hardness of our lot. This is all very
well, but let us be clear about it — the laity have the
really difficult ministry. We in the clergy are protected
by a thousand safeguards. Custom and tradition and
the daily performance thrust on us of holy tasks — all
these cushion our lives. Most of our ministry is the
Church and within the Church, in every sense of that
word. We can speak of familiar things, to people and
among people to whom they are also familiar. The layman has no such easy task. I would not know how to
be a layman now, after thirty years of the priesthood. I

wonder if I could summon up the integrity and the courage it takes to be a layman.

But all this respect for the ministry of the laity, which is very deep and sincere, grows out of one lesson, that the life and work of the layman must be clearly seen, in his own eyes, as something that Christ is doing in him. Whatever work he does, he must do it in the steady remembrance that Christ is doing it. Whatever he does, it must be work which Christ can offer. Whatever work he does, it must be work done so that Christ's Ministry is fulfilled. The witness the layman bears in his work need not be ostentatiously "evangelistic." The layman may have almost as much need of anonymity as the priest does, in this. But what he is really doing must be perfectly clear in his own mind. Far more, it must be a way in which Christ can get His work done in the world, and the world may come to know Christ.

And all this centers and homes at the altar. The layman comes and brings his life, his work and home, his citizenship, and his humanity and puts them into the hands of the minister to offer, that they may be added to the Eternal Sacrifice, and so become the means by which God's children are fed. If a man's job is such that he cannot rightly offer it, then we must look again and more deeply at the job. But may it never be that we fail to make the offering because we think that Christ has nothing to do with it. Far otherwise; it is in the work of the world that Christ's work is chiefly done. Men do not live by bread alone, nor do they live by prayers and hymns alone. What is essential is that a bridge be built between the world and the Church; and it is the peculiar honor and vocation of the laity to build that bridge. But the only way it can be built is by remembering without fail that Christ is the bridge and the bridge-builder. He is the Minister; and through His Ministry, in Church and world, do we find the unity we have lost, and long so deeply to find.

V

"MAY WORTHILY RECEIVE"

". . . that we, and all others who shall be partakers of this Holy Communion, may worthily receive the most precious Body and Blood of thy Son Jesus Christ, be filled with thy grace and heavenly benediction, and made one body with him, that he may dwell in us, and we in him." *

How do we rightly prepare ourselves to take part in the Liturgy and worthily receive the Holy Communion? We have thought about three of the principal eucharistic acts (acts both of God and of the Church, at differing levels and in differing ways) — remembrance, sacrifice, offering. Now what should be said about our personal participation in the Eucharist, which brings the Liturgy to its fulfillment? What ought we think and do, that we "may worthily receive"?

I think at least four things should be said about this.

---

* Like those quoted in Chapter I, these words are found in both the American and Scottish Liturgies in the paragraph "Wherefore O Lord and heavenly Father." In 1662, the opening phrases "O Lord and heavenly Father, we thy humble servants" belong to the "Prayer of Oblation"; the words from "do celebrate . . . ," onwards, though they do not occur in 1662, were adopted from the Scottish Liturgy in the Proposed English Book of 1928, and are used also in other parts of the Anglican Communion.

But in writing these thoughts, I earnestly hope that what I write will not be interpreted as a new manual for communicants. There are many such manuals; and the poorest of them is vastly richer and more inclusive than what follows here. All I mean to do, in this chapter, is to make four comments as to principles.

The first is quite impersonal. It is simply to note that the receiving of the Holy Communion is and should be the rule, and not the exception. This may seem a needless statement, for interested and devout Christians, but it is by no means so. For the greater part of the Church's history, Christians only rarely received the Holy Communion. Sometimes, as in the eighteenth and nineteenth centuries in our Anglican and Episcopalian history, this was so because the Eucharist was only celebrated a few times a year — perhaps quarterly in the typical eighteenth-century parish, and hardly more than monthly in most nineteenth-century situations. But this was exceptional. Far more significant were the long centuries of our medieval history, when the mass was said daily, and still most church people made their communions only once or twice a year. Part of the violent reaction of the Reformation was a reaction against this. And I think the reaction was entirely right, for it seems clear to me that we are intended by our Lord to receive the Holy Communion regularly and frequently, as the usual and expected completion and fulfillment of our share in the whole eucharistic act.

How often the liturgy should be celebrated is a separate question. I can only speak for myself in answering that, to my mind, it should be the principal act of Christian worship every Sunday and on every great day in the Church's year. Indeed I should feel that in a normal parish life, a daily celebration, at an hour which is accessible to most people, probably should be the norm. But if this is to happen, I am sure we must find a way to restore to the Communion service those elements of Biblical and congregational worship which are not now included, but are so richly characteristic of Morning and Evening Prayer. We have an annoying sort of schism in our Church between those who prefer Morning Prayer as the principal service, and those who prefer the Holy Communion. It is wrong to make such a choice; it is wrong to have to make such a choice; there ought not to be any choice to be made, really, for Morning Prayer should be directly related to the Holy Communion, as part of the same life and worship.

As I understand these things, the ante-Communion — the prayers and Bible readings which precede the Offertory — is nothing less than a first cousin of Morning Prayer. Both grew out of the worship of the synagogue, Biblical and congregational as it was, and filled with the participation and response of the laity, centering in the reading of Holy Scripture. But, over the centuries of liturgical history, the reading of Epistle and Gospel and the prayers and Creed became so overshadowed by the great acts which would follow, that they lost the sense of being an act of full congregational worship in favor of a quite different sense of being simply a devotional preparation for the Eucharist. The Old Testament lesson disappeared almost entirely. The psalms have remained only in a permissive rubric which says we can sing "a Hymn or an Anthem" between the Epistle and the Gospel, if we wish. The prayers now are reduced, usually, only to the Collect for purity, the Kyrie and the proper Collect for the day. And all of it is generally so overladen with the essential priestliness of the great acts to follow, that there is little sense of the gathering of the household of God to hear the Word of God and join in the corporate praises of God.

This sense of simple, Biblical, corporate worship more and more has become attached to the choir offices, to Morning and Evening Prayer. And thus it has become a matter of choice; and to many church people, Morning Prayer is definitely preferable, as an act of corporate worship, to the Holy Communion — at least as far as general use is concerned. The Eucharist then tends to be thought of as an occasional service, to be used at an early hour for the especially devout, or on special occasions (but please, not Easter, because it takes so long and people can't kneel in a crowd, and anyway too many of the congregation will be people who would be embarrassed by the Blessed Sacrament or think it was "high church" etc.).

I think such talk is nonsense, and I wish that no such choice had to confront us; but the problem is a real one. It is a fact that Morning Prayer is, in many ways, a more satisfactory act of corporate worship than the Eucharist; it is true that even our reformed liturgy, beautiful as it is, is still heavily burdened with clericalism, and becomes a pious monologue; it is true that Morning Prayer now has a healthy and vivid sense of Biblical and moral reality which the Holy Communion service does not so clearly have; and I cannot blame anybody for thinking of Morning Prayer as the "regular service," and of the Eucharist as an immensely holy and mysterious, but most obscure and recherché kind of service, much beloved of clergymen and pious people but without the warmth and outwardness and witness we wish the Church's services to have.

The answer to this is not to damn the choice, but to make it unnecessary. There should be not such schism within our worship. The Eucharist is the one specifically Christian act of worship, one of the only two services our Lord definitely told us to do (the other being Holy Baptism). It should always be the normal and characteristic service whenever Christian people gather for worship. But it should include all that Morning Prayer gives us, and the spirit of Morning Prayer; and until it does, we shall have to accommodate ourselves to the choice. Indeed it helps, in the American Prayer Book, to have the permissive shortening of Morning Prayer when it is used before the Holy Communion, which lets us, after the Canticle following the first lesson, go at once to the Holy Communion. At least this supplies the element of Old Testament scripture reading. But this permission is no answer to the main problem; it makes a poor bobtailed thing out of Morning Prayer without helping to give the Holy Sacrifice those elements of corporate participation it needs; and we are still left with an unhappy feeling that there are two levels of worship in the Prayer Book, and that we probably like the wrong one.

Forgive this long detour, which is not really entirely irrelevant. My first main point is that, normally and rightly, the Eucharist is not complete without our participation in the Holy Communion. To this, many will be moved to ask "why?" Is it not enough to share in the great acts without necessarily being personally involved in the communion? Is there nothing to be gained simply from kneeling in awe and reverence during the holy Mysteries, and sharing in them through some act of spiritual communion?

Of course, there is something to be gained — and sometimes everything to be gained — from such an act of spiritual communion. There are times when it would be quite inappropriate for us to receive the Blessed Sacrament. For example, any of us may find ourselves in the situation where there is only a Roman Catholic celebration to attend; and I think it would be wrong for us to receive the Sacrament at their hands, except in unusual circumstances, knowing that we are excommunicate in their eyes. I would not hesitate to ask to receive the Sacrament in case of some emergency; but as a matter of steady discipline, it is far truer to ourselves and our self-respect and our respect for the consciences of other Christian people, to refrain from receiving at their altars; and in such a case, God does not punish us because we have not made a sacramental communion. Indeed He may even deepen and strengthen our life through the offering of an austerity willingly and understandingly accepted.

Or again, it happens that we are prevented from making any adequate preparation to receive the Holy Communion, by reason of some unexpected obligation or lateness or confusion; and how much wiser it is for us then simply to be carried for a little while on the shoulders of the attentive devotion of other Christians, until we are ready ourselves once again to take our own part.

No, it is sometimes quite enough to share in the Eucharist without receiving the elements. But these times are exceptions. The inescapable goal toward which the Liturgy moves is our own sharing in the sacramental Body and Blood. It is this which He commanded — "Take, eat" — it is this which finally unites us with Him and our offering with His. We are not angels; we are men and women whose life is inescapably bound up with things, with time and space, bread and wine, and bodies and blood. There is no use our pretending to be pure spirit. It may be that sometime we will be set free from this imprisonment (if that is what it is), but that time is not now; and for now, this is the way He has chosen to make Himself known to us. Therefore we have not the right to scorn it. Rather we accept His command, and our own creatureliness, and are content to be fed inwardly through these humble outward things.

More, we accept the command to be involved. Not a little of so-called "spirituality" is fake spirituality; it is a deliberate attempt to avoid being involved in man's history. Many, perhaps even a majority of the people of this earth, follow religions whose end is to show them how to escape being involved in this world, how to cease caring and loving and being hurt and making choices wise or foolish. But this is not what Christ came to do or to teach. He did not seek to escape history or time or space Himself. The Cross is the indelible mark of God's will to be involved in the world. Christ came to show us how to live as the children of God should live in the world, and to use it, and conquer it by His good grace. And one of the supreme symbols of that involvement is that we deliberately, thoughtfully, come forward to receive the broken bread and the cup, in company with all of the others.

"The Sacraments were not ordained of Christ to be gazed upon, or to be carried about, but that we should duly use them" (Article XXV). The Eucharist is not something to be watched, it is an act to be shared. And the principal means of the sharing is through the communion. It is toward this that the whole immense structure of the Liturgy moves. And we are not to loiter piously afterwards either. There is and should be only a minimum of devotion to follow our communions — our our personal thanksgiving, as warm and fervent as can be; the corporate thanksgiving of the congregation; a corporate act of praise; then a dismissal. For myself, I must own to a distaste even for the traditional blessing which ends the service. As I grow older, I feel more and more foolish to be tacking on this hallowed effrontery, after the Lord Himself has blessed us with His Body; and if I were in charge, I would command that this bit of medieval, clerical ostentation be done away. I want to be quiet for a minute, and then soberly join with my brethren in thanksgiving, then get out of the practice world of the church into the world outside, where I must live out all this that I have seen and shared. It is distracting to have blessings and prayers and choir processions and devotions bellowed from the sacristy. It is a good thing I am not in charge of the Church.

But it is good that we begin our thoughts of worthy reception of the Holy Communion by accepting the fact that to receive the Sacrament is the reason why it is given to us. That is where we must begin.

Secondly, because we are personally involved in the Sacrifice, it is needful that we join in it with as clean hands as God can give us. This is a way of talking about the direct preparation we ought to make for our Holy Communion. The Prayer Book, several times, lays out the general outline of what this preparation should be. The Office of Instruction (p. 293) teaches us "it is required of those who come to the Lord's Supper to examine themselves, whether they repent them truly of their former sins, with stedfast purpose to lead a new life; to have a lively faith in God's mercy through Christ, with a thankful remembrance of his death; and to be in charity with all men."

A classic elaboration of these principles is found in the first Exhortation (p. 85), especially in these words ". . . repent you truly for your sins past; have a lively and stedfast faith in Christ our Saviour; amend your lives, and be in perfect charity with all men; . . . above all things ye must give most humble and hearty thanks to God, the Father, the Son, and the Holy Ghost, for the redemption of the world by the death and passion of our Saviour Christ, both God and man. . . ." The second Exhortation (pp. 86–88) teaches how this self-examination is to be done, and what it should require of us. So too, in lovely simplicity, the Invitation says "Ye who do truly and earnestly repent you of your sins, and are in love and charity with your neighbours, and intend to lead a new life, following the commandments of God, and walking from henceforth in his holy ways; Draw near with faith. . . ."

All these alike speak of the four essential ingredients of true preparation — repentance, love, faith, thanksgiving. And through them all must run the deep stream of honesty and humility. Repentance does not mean saying to God that we don't quite know how but we are sure we have done something wrong, nor does it mean trying to attract His attention to how horrible we are, and how much better than anybody else we are because we know how horrible we are. Repentance is an honest, humble acknowledgment of the ways in which we have deliberately disobeyed God's will, or if not deliberately, have come to see afterwards how we did disobey and should have known better. Repentance is not a general misery. It is based on such knowledge of ourselves as we presently have, of our growth, of our needs, if we are to be what God created us to be. It must be honest, for otherwise it is nothing but superstitious words. It must be humble, because otherwise it is not a repentance for our sins, but rather a left-handed boasting about them. Honesty in self-examination comes from a willingness to accept the fact that no sin is unforgivable, provided we really mean business about our repentance for it. Humility comes from a willingness to face the fact that nobody, including ourselves, is very loving or very big or very strong, but that we are all created to be those things.

Mostly, I think, we need to expect to be changed — to be forgiven, and to move on to new problems and new possibilities. It does little good to be told that we are sinners and always will be. I know that I am; and it may be that I shall always be; but it is my *particular* sins that I must cope with, if God is ever to take my sinfulness away. When I was twenty, my sins were different than what they are now. They were different yesterday than today. And if I am not prepared to be that honest and that humble that I can confess what I really did or left undone, then there isn't much point in going on with great generalities about my sinfulness as a whole.

This kind of self-examination is the least morbid of all human activities. What would be morbid and untrue and hypocritical, would be for me to say "Oh yes, I am sure I am wicked" (or to say "I think God is too big to care about my little peccadilloes," which is really another way of saying the same thing). This would be a sickness of the soul maybe even beyond God's power to heal. But when, in wholesome perspective and self-knowledge, we make our daily pilgrimage with God, expecting to be different day by day, hoping to be stronger and gentler and truer, willing to have Him know us and heal us, this is the heart of true repentance. This is no morbid egotism; it is always an act of love, not of fear. It is love for God which leads us to it, and love for our neighbor which makes us long to be more nearly what we ought to be.

And love grows out of repentance as well as leading to it. D. T. Niles said "Evangelism is one hungry man telling another hungry man where food is to be found." Apply this to forgiveness, if you will. One of us has found forgiveness. His deepest impulse is to give it to somebody else. The Prayer Book is very practical about this. Love is not something restricted to your emotions, in the Prayer Book. It is, first of all, something you do. A man and woman marrying promise to love each other. And if they are sensible (which they usually are not, at the moment) they know that there will be many times when their acts of consideration and understanding will need to go on, even though resentment and hurt is very near the surface. Love of God is equally matter-of-fact — to love Him means to express that love in acts, of worship, of thanks, of trust, of reverence, of service.

So it is with our neighbors. The second Exhortation puts it thus: "And if ye shall perceive your offences to be such as are not only against God, but also against your neighbours; then ye shall reconcile yourselves unto them; being ready to make restitution and satisfaction, according to the uttermost of your powers, for all injuries and wrongs done by you to any other; and being likewise ready to forgive others who have offended you. . . ." Repentance leads to love as well as growing out of it. But just as healthy penitence is infinitely more than merely a general gloom about one's self, so is love more than a vague feeling of benevolence. Both alike are things *done* more than things *felt*. At least they are, where they are not morbid and inverted.

So it is with the two other preparatory acts taught by the Prayer Book — faith and thanksgiving. Here again, the danger of purely subjective and indeed egotistical thinking is very real. Faith is a duty, so the Prayer Book says ("my duty towards God is to believe in Him . . ."); and an emotional conviction cannot be a duty. I cannot promise to be sure of God anymore than I can promise to feel loving toward my neighbor. What I can promise is to commit myself to God in the way I live and choose, so far as I have that much freedom and self-control. We have all of us noticed, in saying the Creed, that we are not so much expressing a matter of intellectual credence (although we are that, too) as we are saying, in effect, "I bet my life on God." This bet, this self-commitment, is what the New Testament almost invariably means by "faith." It is an act of the will, of course; it is the final determination of the free man to devote himself and his decisions to the best thing he knows.

So again with thanksgiving. If there are particular and personal blessings to be grateful about, so much the better. And there usually are, if we look. But do not the publicans the same? What "Eucharist" means, and what the Prayer Book means when it says "above all things ye must give most humble and hearty thanks to God . . . ," is not just that we shall duly purr when life has been kind to us. What is meant is that we shall unfailingly remember the gigantic acts of God, in our creation, our salvation, our continuing life with Him and in Him — that we shall remember and steadily wonder at the incredible miracle of our existence in God's universe, and remembering, come thankfully to acknowledge all He has done and is doing and will do, and the glory of it.

This is the Eucharist, this steady remembrance of the fact of God and of His unfailing being and love. And this thanksgiving is the final act of preparation.

Repentance, love, faith, all lead up to the sober remembrance of the God Who is in all this and behind it and working through it, and this remembrance means thanksgiving — the basic ground of all Christian living. Thanksgiving is the thoughtful man's answer to God's love for him. It becomes the central axis of his life. Duty, love, penitence, self-control . . . all the acts of Christian life grow out of this fundamental orientation of man toward God, for which the word is thanksgiving. It is an attitude of mind and of will; it is a deliberate exercise in self-discipline and in the direction of one's life; like faith, which is the way thanksgiving expresses itself in action, it is the high point of responsible freedom in us.

I have perhaps made all this sound terribly cold. If so, I have been misleading, for I do not disdain the emotional aspects of our religion, nor think them unimportant or irrelevant. Still I have lived long enough to know that we are not simply the creatures of our emotions but in large part also the creators of them. I have lived long enough to know that what I do determines what I shall feel, far more often than the other way around. There is no marriage in human history which would endure a year if there were not duty in it. Faithfulness and loyalty are acts before they are feelings. A citizen is not a good citizen because he blandly agrees with all his country does and is; he is a good citizen precisely because he does his duty no matter what he feels about it at the time. Christians need to remember the word "duty," that obedience which is perfect freedom, according to our faith.

But when duty is done, joy and peace follow it as day follows dark. This is the usual order of things in our imperfect world. I dare say that in heaven it will not necessarily be so — there a man's feelings and a man's acts will be one and the same, as it is with God, because we will be united inside ourselves, and our freedom will be perfect because we will be wholehearted in our love of God. In this imperfect world a man must choose all this, and choose it often amid a confusion of other possibilities. Yet we may choose it; and on this choice of duty and of the always-costly obedience on which freedom depends, lies the heart of what it is to be human.

So the Prayer Book teaches us, and holds before us the picture of the sober, responsible man or woman, coming to the holy Mysteries in penitence and love, in faith and thanksgiving, prepared to make a real offering of self to God in certain confidence that such an offering is the most, indeed the only, acceptable offering we can make. And with that offering comes the abiding joy and peace which are God's gifts to those who love Him with all their hearts and minds and souls and strength.

Third, there is an element of expectancy in all this preparation, which is a curiously forgotten ingredient in our devotions. There is a recurring danger of "liturgical paralysis" in Christian history. One example of this is the strangely static character of many medieval communion devotions. The early Christian hymns about the Holy Communion were often hymns having to do with what God was accomplishing, or wanted to accomplish in the worshippers, in the Church, through the Liturgy. Two of the oldest hymns in our American hymnal are of that character. "Father, we thank thee who hast planted thy holy name within our hearts" (Hymn 195) is one of the most ancient of liturgical hymns, and is a hymn basically about the way God wills to preserve the unity of the Church through the Eucharist. "As grain, once scattered on the hillsides, was in this broken bread made one, so from all lands thy Church be gathered into thy Kingdom by thy Son." So is it with another classic hymn, "Draw nigh and take the Body of the Lord, and drink the holy Blood for you outpoured" (Hymn 202) a seventh-century hymn about how God comes into our world and our life through His sacrifice, and offers us the privilege to share in that sacrifice, day by day.

These are examples, I should think, of the truest kind of communion devotion. But many of the later hymns, written in a time of infrequent reception of the

Holy Communion, turn away from this dynamic approach to a more passive one. The great hymns of St. Thomas Aquinas — "Humbly I adore thee, Verity unseen" (204), "Now, my tongue, the mystery telling of the glorious Body sing" (199), "O saving Victim, opening wide the gate of heaven to man below" (209) †
— such hymns, which are classics indeed, seem written in a mood only of wondering awe at a mighty deed done long ago or far away. They are hymns of profound solemnity, celebrating the immense miracle of the Liturgy and the Sacrifice, yet often omitting any reference to the part man has in this divine transaction, or how he may and must appropriate God's gifts.

These strike me as instances of the mood of passivity, of liturgical paralysis, which descended all too often on medieval devotion. And even though the Reformers were acutely aware of the need for a new sense of human response, still many of the great Reformation hymns are likely to be of the same character. True, rather than meditating about the mystery of transubstantiation, they are likely to meditate about the wonder of God's love on the Cross so long ago. But in this they are often equally unclear about any responsible human participa-

---

† Versions of the hymns here quoted from the American Episcopal *Hymn Book* occur in other Anglican books, for example *English Hymnal* (331, 236, 330 [part 2]), *Ancient and Modern* (312, 309, 311 [part 2]), *Ancient and Modern Revised* (385, 383, 384, [part 2]).

tion in God's acts. We have almost none of this type of hymn in our hymnal. One of the loveliest, which happily we do have, is Franck's "Deck thyself, my soul, with gladness, leave the gloomy haunts of sadness" (210),‡ which rises above the passivity of so many contemporary hymns. But in many of the collections of seventeenth- and eighteenth-century Protestant hymns, this same note of passivity is very strong.

I am not arguing against the element of adoration and wonder, far from it. But I am sure that any eucharistic devotion is incomplete which does not finally bring us into a dynamic, responsible relationship with what is being done by God in the great Sacrament. Probably the most deeply loved of our hymns is Bright's "And now, O Father, mindful of the love that bought us, once for all, on Calvary's tree . . ." (189).§ This is not only a deservedly loved hymn; to me it is one of the classic statements of eucharistic theology. And it moves from remembrance and wonder and awe to active prayer, and then to our participation — "And so we come; O draw us to thy feet, most patient Saviour, who canst love us still! And by this food, so awful and so sweet, deliver us from every touch of ill: In thine own service make us glad and free, and grant us nevermore

---

‡ *English Hymnal*, 306; *Ancient and Modern Revised*, 393 at the hymn reference (189):—
§ *E.H.* 302; *A. & M.* 322; *A. & M. R.*, 397.

to part with thee." This is as succinct a statement of participation in the Eucharist as I know.

Now this is not simply an excursus on hymns. What I want to say is that part of our preparation of ourselves that we "may worthily receive," is to break out of a paralyzed and passive wonder, into a readiness to take our part in what God is doing and means to do. This requires of us a willingness to expect God to do something real in us. Or, to say it another way, it means that the offering we make is always the same, yet is never the same two days running. It is always the same because all we have to offer is ourselves, and from our first communion to our death there is a continuous self, held together by memory, which makes an offering of itself. Yet, precisely because we do offer ourselves, therefore it is always ourselves as we are, where we are. And this is never the same.

What we offer is what we are that day — our past, up to that point — the choices we are facing at that moment — our needs, as we then know them — our hopes as clearly as we can see them at the time. And how utterly unreal it would be if we were not aware of changing needs, of new hopes, of a fresh offering every day. The worst thing that can happen to us in life is to lose the expectancy of being different. This is the misery and death of the soul, when a man or woman resigns himself to a defeated, static cynicism about ever being different than what he is. When this happens, Christian faith ceases to have any real meaning for us. It becomes a cemetery of dead hopes, of defeated resolutions. But this is not at all what Christ means us to feel.

One of the surest lessons of Christian life is that there is no time limit on God's mercy. There is no statute of limitations on conversion. The last day of a man's life is as new and as filled with promise as the day he was born. And the Holy Communion is built precisely on this truth. The love of God in Christ, that love which expressed itself "once for all on Calvary's tree," is an unchanging fact about God. At each celebration "We here present, we here spread forth" to God "that only offering perfect in Thine eyes." And then we go on to make that love ours, to let God love us and win us and change us and hold us as He eternally means to do. He will not rest content, His love will not be fulfilled, until He has won us to Himself.

Therefore life is a continuing pilgrimage with God, toward God, never the same because we are never the same nor in the same place. And our communions are the great moments when we draw closest to Him in our pilgrimage, offering all we can offer at that moment, then going on in the power of God to a new offering tomorrow, which may, in God's mercy, be a little more complete, a little more full and free than what we could offer Him today.

This, then, is the third note of preparation, that we shall expect a new start and a new self. In the words of the Invitation, we come to the Holy Communion "intending to lead a new life." If we do not believe such a thing to be possible, then the Eucharist will forever be a distant, mysterious transaction unrelated to us, calling perhaps for amazement and fear, but holding no room for us and issuing no invitation to us to share in it. If we expect this new life which God can give, and intend it and seek it, then the Lord's Supper will be the recurring moment when we bring what we have and what we are to His feet, and ask Him in His mercy to put it into the hands of the Father, from Whom it came.

Finally, I ask what is the meaning of such a phrase as the one I just used — "Put our life into the hands of the Father, from Whom it came"? Is it anything more than a preacher's phrase, designed to evoke an emotional image of some kind? Is it not really a description of a kind of suicide, a self-annihilation? How can a man or woman serve God by giving up, losing, whatever he has or is? And if what is offered is not real, then what is the sense of the act of offering? Is it then anything but a mystical exercise of some sort, unrelated to our day-by-day life except as a kind of emotional token of something quite outside our ken?

There is an answer to these questions, and the answer is perhaps the most important part of preparing worthily to receive the sacrament. The answer has already been suggested in some of the things we have thought about offering, and its centrality in the Christian life. The answer lies in the final principle of offering, *that we are fed with what we have offered*. Our Lord spoke of such a thing when He said that "He that loseth his life for my sake and the gospel's, shall find it." True, he was not speaking of the Eucharist, but of a general principle of life. But the Eucharist is simply life raised to its highest level; and what is true at any level is supremely true at the summit. We receive what we give. We are fed by what we have offered.

It is so, first of all, in the bread and wine which the celebrant offers and places on the altar. In some churches, it is so arranged that as each communicant enters, he or she takes a wafer of bread from a bowl near the door, and at the Offertory comes forward to place his own wafer on the paten. This is no more than a little, vivid, acted parable, and no great importance attaches to it. But it seems to underline how it is that what we give, we receive. The consecrated bread and wine are no other than the same elements which were ours to grow, ours to manufacture, ours to give. We do give them, and then we are fed by them. After Christ has received them, offered them, and added them to His sacrifice, He in turn gives us back what we gave, made whatever He chooses to make it, to feed us.

But all this is no more than an outward and visible sign, a sign of His Body and Blood and of the benefits we receive from that holy Supper. His Body and Blood is the reality which fills the sign with meaning. So, precisely, is it with the personal gifts we have offered, those tokens of money or time, of word and deed. It is by them that we are fed; but when they are returned to us, they are made what He wills them to be — filled with the reality He intends to give to them.

What I mean is very simple. A man has to live with what he is and has — his time, his talents, his particular opportunities and choices, the circumstances of his own life. In the face of the vast needs of humanity, in the face of his own great hopes, even the best offering he can make is ridiculously small. A few years, a tiny talent, a little money, a ridiculously mixed set of motives. . . . "What are these among so many?" They aren't much, to tell the truth. Nobody has very much to offer.

Yet it is by these things that we must live. We haven't any other life to live; it must be these offerings we shall make, or none. And when we realize this, it is hard not to despair. What priest, facing the endless need and pain of the people to whom he ministers, does not despair at times — how can his pathetically small and impure offering possibly meet those needs? What parent, longing to give the best things to his children, does not know heartbreak at how little he really can give them? What citizen, looking at the weakness and dividedness of his own life, does not tremble at the urgent requirements of citizenship in our world and weep at how little he can bring to that task?

And when a preacher says to us, knowing all these things about ourselves, that it is by these imperfect offerings that we shall be fed, who is to blame for doubting or ridiculing the whole theology of offering? It would be a starvation diet! And so it would, if it were not for one thing — the way He takes our offerings and makes them what He wills them to be.

The bread and wine of the Holy Communion are very little things. If we were to depend on them for anything more than symbolic nourishment, they would not be much use to us. Yet we do see how they become the vessels of a grace and power quite adequate to make heroes and saints out of people like ourselves. Why should we marvel, then, at what God makes out of the other offerings we give Him? Suppose it is true that a man has only a little time he can offer to God. Does this mean then that God is equally limited in what He can use that time for? Do we not remember that sometimes a man lives for twenty years for the sake of one hour of courage or love? If our earthly scale of values were all that counted, what would we make of Christ's thirty-three years?

No, we cannot judge the final worth of what we offer. In humility and penitence, we make the best oblation we can, knowing it is not what we wish it were, not enough. Yet it is by this offering that we shall be fed and shall live. A man offers his imperfect priesthood, a woman her little talent, a family their tiny means, a businessman his limited and harassed service, an artist such skill as he has . . . and these offerings are all we have and are. They are our life and we must live by them, in them, and no other. But suddenly, wonderfully, God transforms them, uses them; and a certain strange dignity and worth pervades them, little as they are. They do not change, in themselves; but the use God makes of them is what tells the story. Like the eucharistic bread that is always bread, that simple and plain thing, so do our work and love and talents stay what they are. But, like the sacramental signs, suddenly this does not matter — there is more given to us through them than we could possibly understand or grasp.

This is precisely what mankind learns about life, when it is freely and trustingly offered. The life of a priest, limited and imperfect as it is, suddenly becomes so great a thing that if we lived a thousand years we could not fulfill it, exhaust it, deserve it. The life of the mother or father, so utterly inadequate to the needs, suddenly is turned into a partnership so rich that we cannot even begin to imagine it. So with the work of all our hands and minds, so with our time and money, so with our words and meetings and friendships, so with all we offer. We are fed with what we offer, and it is enough.

The title of Bishop Bayne's new book is taken from William Bright's eucharistic hymn, "And now, O Father, mindful of the love." In his characteristic style, Bishop Bayne gives the reader a straightforward explanation of the meaning of the Holy Communion and its effects in the daily life of the Christian. An outgrowth of the Mc-Math Lecture series, sponsored by the Diocese of Michigan of the Episcopal Church, this book is primarily intended for the instruction of lay people. It will, however, also help clergy to understand eucharistic theology on deep levels. Bishop Bayne's reference to the Episcopal Book of Common Prayer does not rule out the very wide application of his remarks. Thus, non-Anglicans will discover much of interest to their position.

The book develops five different aspects of the Eucharist and is not too technical theologically: "Having in Remembrance"; "Our Sacrifice of Praise and Thanksgiving"; "Here We Offer"; "We, Thy Humble Servants"; and "May Worthily Receive." To quote from the author's Foreword,